A History *of* LONGFELLOW'S

Wayside Inn

BRIAN E. PLUMB

Charleston   London

THE
History
PRESS

Published by The History Press
Charleston, SC 29403
www.historypress.net

Cover: From an F.A. Strauss etching of Thomas Hill's 1870 painting *Wayside Inn*. This painting is on display at the inn.

Unless otherwise noted, all photos in this book are from the archives of the Wayside Inn and are used with permission. All pictures are copyrighted by the inn or others.

First published 2011

Manufactured in the United States

ISBN 978.1.60949.396.7

Library of Congress Cataloging-in-Publication Data

Plumb, Brian E.
A history of Longfellow's Wayside Inn / Brian E. Plumb.
p. cm.
Includes bibliographical references.
ISBN 978-1-60949-396-7
1. Wayside Inn (Sudbury, Mass.)--History. I. Title.
TX941.W38P58 2011
910.4609744'4--dc23
2011037865

CONTENTS

The Wayside Inn in 1880 with a busload of tourists (down near the tree to the left). *Courtesy of the Sudbury Historical Society.*

PREFACE

Travel in the days of yore brought with it both exhaustion and danger. At best, the roads were well-trodden dirt paths—dusty, isolated and unprotected. The weary traveler had to feel relieved seeing the next tavern on the road ahead.

These were the days when wayside taverns were absolutely essential to travel, communications and the transportation of most goods. Their era was a long one, roughly a 220-year period from the colonial days of 1630 to the coming of the iron horse. As commerce routes and the pace of life in America changed, the modern "hotel" became the refuge travelers sought. Some taverns tried to adapt to these more modern times, their graceful architecture sacrificed to efficiency; others just disappeared. A few, fortunately, survived, and a rare few have even continued to operate.

Given its colonial past, it is no surprise that several old taverns still exist around the Boston area. Some of the less distinguished ones have been beautifully restored as private homes. The more prominent ones, such as the Buckman and Munroe Taverns in Lexington, the Hartwell Tavern in Lincoln and the Golden Ball Tavern in Weston, are restored as museums and are opened seasonally to the public.

The grandest and most venerable of all the historic taverns still standing is the ancient Wayside Inn of Sudbury, Massachusetts. Its three-hundred-year history goes back to the days of Indian affairs and colonial wars. It witnessed the birth of the nation, as well as the coming of the stagecoach, railroad and automobile. Great patriots of every generation have passed over its threshold. The poet Henry Wadsworth Longfellow immortalized it in verse, and Henry Ford touched it with his wealth. It stands open today, still serving both man and beast. While the inn's rich history alone sets it apart, its physical presence is just as remarkable. The striking vernacular architecture and its harmonious placement in the landscape give it that transcendental feel that very few buildings in the world possess.

My first visit to the Wayside Inn came on a cold October night twenty-five years ago. As I approached, I could smell the fire burning and see its red glow "gleaming" through the window, just as Longfellow described. I pushed open the large black front door (an original relic from the past), and there it was—it was like stepping back in time. To the left was Longfellow's famous Parlor of his *Tales*. To the right was the ancient Bar Room. The fire was burning warmly in the large open fireplace, and the music of fife and drum was in the air. Exposed beams, pewter mugs, antique English caricature prints and the wide plank floor gave the room its full character. The old bar, "with the railed portcullis, which rose to the call of refreshments, or fell as trade was dull"—a description reiterated in so many magazines articles from the past—stood in the corner. Walking through the rest of the inn, I knew there was a story to be told.

Indeed, it had been. While the oral tradition had long carried on the story, in 1874 Samuel Adams Drake, a noted historian of the time, devoted several pages to the inn in his book *Historic Fields and Mansions of Middlesex*. In 1889, Alfred S. Hudson included a six-page highlight of the inn in his oft-referenced *History of Sudbury*. Later, in 1897, Samuel Bent put together the first full-summarized history of the inn, to that point, in the form of a speech given to the Society of Colonial Wars. Numerous turn-of-the-century articles drawing from these earlier works were later published. It then took until 1988 for an updated and more accurate history to be written. Curtis Garfield and his wife, Alison Ridley (archivist at the inn in the late 1980s), put together the well-researched book *As Ancient Is This Hostelry: The Story of the Wayside Inn*. All this book lacked were photos and the power of the Internet to help pull in further research. I thought there was possibly an opportunity to tell the tale in a slightly different, and perhaps more accessible, way.

Predating the thought of writing a book, I started a website—howetavern. com—to begin sharing my growing collection of inn photos, stories and other resources. I also wanted to capture and put into the public record the knowledge and documents our generation has accumulated so nothing was lost or forgotten. Since websites do not last forever, a book seemed the logical next step to preserve this record and bring the story to more people. The board of trustees of the Wayside Inn, which had already been considering an updated book about the inn, wholeheartedly agreed and opened the archives for this book's research.

With respect to the archives, like any record of history, they are incomplete. You cannot record everything, and you cannot keep everything recorded.[1] There is no known history of the inn prior to the 1870s in written form. Writers from the late nineteenth century undoubtedly relied in some part on oral tradition to create their histories. Longfellow, for example, spoke to a Miss Eaton at the inn. She showed the poet the How family relics, gave him a tour and provided him with her version of the history. Drake obtained his story and facts from somewhere; he must have interviewed people with knowledge of the inn (he did in fact interview Longfellow). It is entirely possible that written documents once existed with the ancient history. Adam Howe, the third landlord, was said to be a historian. Unfortunately, none of this history survives in the inn's records. This ancient history could still exist somewhere, perhaps buried in someone's attic or glued to the back of some old picture frame. If it ever does get discovered, it would make for a fascinating "definitive history" someday.

Records from the early days that do exist are in the form of deeds, licenses, account books, wills and other town records. A very limited number of firsthand accounts in the form of letters, reminiscences, rare photos and brief published articles have also been preserved. Some of this information came fairly recently to the inn as part of a very generous donation in 1995 by the Herbert Howe family. Using the material in the archives and the knowledge of the few remaining "inn experts" still around, I was able to piece together this story.

A few acknowledgements are required. Thanks foremost to Antoinette (Toni) Frederick, the inn's archivist. Without her knowledge, research assistance, friendship and flexibility in coordinating access to the inn's archives, this book could never have been written. Thanks to the board of trustees; its chairman, Joe Vrabel; and the innkeeper, John Cowden, for giving me the opportunity to write this book. Thanks to The History Press and my editor, Jeff Saraceno, for all their help and support. Thanks to Richard Gnatowski, the inn's miller, and Guy LeBlanc, the director of marketing and historical services at the inn, for their insights and photo contributions. I also want to thank and acknowledge Lee Swanson and Robert Kane of the Sudbury and Marlborough, Massachusetts (respectively) Historical Societies for their help and also for all the effort they put into preserving their towns' histories. Thanks to Al Petty, Lynn Bjorklund, Dr. Tony Howes, Russ and Carol Kirby and Dan and Betty Moylan for sharing their knowledge of the inn. Finally, I am indebted to my wife, Catherine, and my colleagues Deirdre Sweeney, Greg Rice and Ann Koppeis Bowles for their additional insights on the inn and for their reviews and comments on the manuscript.

INTRODUCTION

An honest tale speeds best, being plainly told.
—William Shakespeare

A long the Post Road, in "a sequestered nook among the hills," as Drake writes, stands the old hostelry known today as Longfellow's Wayside Inn. Three hundred years ago, it was called the How Tavern, and for the first 150 of these years, business flourished. Sudbury as a town benefited from its very fortunate location, being roughly twenty miles from both Boston and the next largest city west, Worcester. By 1790, improvements in stagecoach design and competition drove stage operators to change horse teams every twenty miles, instead of every six to ten miles as in the past. Sudbury seemed to be well situated to capitalize on this opportunity. *Badger and Porter's Stage Register*, the bimonthly bible of stage and steam travel schedules in its day, shows that in March 1829 alone, nine coaches were stopping in town daily.[2]

The How Tavern was not the oldest tavern in town—that claim goes to the Parmenter Tavern, circa 1653 (now long gone)—nor was it the only one on Sudbury's section of the Post Road. An 1830 map shows three taverns: the J. Rice Tavern in the Mill Village part of South Sudbury, the Wm. Stone Tavern a mile west of it and How's Tavern two miles farther.[3] The How Tavern was, however, the oldest establishment in town west of the Sudbury River and likely the best kept and most capacious of all local taverns. From it ran roads to Framingham and Sudbury Center. An 1888 newspaper says of the inn: "Being almost literally a half-way house [between Worcester and Boston], it was a

Looking north, the inn is seen in the middle between the barns. The road in the foreground leads to Framingham and was called Wayside Inn Road before 1928. This road runs into the Boston Post Road, which traverses east–west between the barns and the house. Undated photo, likely 1860s.

favorite stopping place for wayfarers."[4] Very large horse barns in old photos also suggest that the tavern picked up a fair amount of the stage business.

There was one other attraction to this tavern: it was run by a family of prominence in the community who likely knew the politics and business of the day. This family went by the name of How (or Howe, the "e" being used interchangeably in the 1700s and then added permanently by the mid-1800s). From the seventeenth to the nineteenth centuries, from the age of King Phillip to the time of the Civil War, the Hows owned this land. Each generation passed it to the next—Samuel (b. 1642) to his son David How (b. 1674, who built the tavern), to Ezekiel (b. 1720), to Adam (b. 1763), to Lyman (b. 1801). In 1868, a newspaper writer familiar with the last two generations wrote, "Indeed, none but those reared in one of our quiet rural towns can appreciate the importance attached to a family possessed of the wealth and independence of the Howe family."[5]

The full tale really starts two generations before the inn was even built. David's grandfather John How (b. 1602) started this noble How lineage when he came from England in the 1630s. With great fortitude and determination, he headed into the wilderness, chopped down trees, built roads and literally and figuratively helped build this country from nothing. He played a large role in settling two Massachusetts towns, Sudbury and Marlborough. John also later kept a tavern in Marlborough, starting the How innkeeper tradition. His son Samuel kept a tavern in Sudbury about six miles from the Wayside Inn site. It was Samuel who deeded the Wayside Inn land to his son David, and it was David who later built the first tavern.

Originally, it was known as How's Tavern "of Sudbury" to distinguish it from a few other How family taverns in neighboring Marlborough. It has also been referred to as Howe's Tavern, How's, How's Place and How's Hotel. At some point between the late 1700s and mid-1800s, it picked up the additional trade name as the Red Horse Tavern, although the family name still seemed to be used throughout its early life. For many reasons, the prosperous times of the tavern came to an end by 1861. The tavern was inherited by an aunt and kept in her family for thirty-two years. During this time, it was no longer a tavern; rather, it was a rented country home for three consecutive tenants. Stabilizing repairs were made, but the structure lacked any real improvements.

The beginning of this tenant period coincided with the publication of Henry Wadsworth Longfellow's *Tales of a Wayside Inn* in 1863. This book of verse, set at the tavern in Sudbury, became an instant bestseller. With the book's publicity, so came publicity for the inn. Just like the old Tabard Inn in Geoffrey Chaucer's *Canterbury Tales*, the Sudbury tavern found itself immortalized.

It is interesting that Longfellow's book of verse was really not even about the Wayside Inn; rather, it was a collection of tales told by seven friends sitting around the fire of the inn's front parlor. The inn, like the pilgrimage of the *Canterbury Tales*, was just a literary vehicle used to develop these other stories. Fortunately, and quite elegantly, Longfellow introduces the tavern to us through his poem's three Preludes. We are given poetic images of such things as a red horse sign, a stone bridge, a picture of a princess and a rhythm on a windowpane. These and other images he provided captured people's hearts and imaginations. Visitors came to the inn wanting to see for themselves the romantic setting that had so inspired the great poet.

Longfellow also did not call the inn the Wayside Inn as a formal name. His book was *Tales of a Wayside Inn*. His use of "wayside" was as an adjective. He was simply referring to a typical inn found along the wayside. Since the opening verse in the first Prelude was called THE WAYSIDE INN, it is no surprise that colloquial usage just swapped this romantic-sounding adjective/noun out for the old name. The identity it had for roughly 180 years as the How Tavern and then the Red Horse Tavern gave way. By 1897, it permanently became Longfellow's Wayside Inn.

Besides Longfellow and his poem, another event of that era would have a meaningful but less direct impact on the inn: the Civil War. In 1863, major battles were still being fought (Gettysburg and Vicksburg, among others). When the war finally ended in 1865, the trauma and victory it brought manifested a new sense of patriotism, which, along with the centennial of this country coming a few years later in 1876, reinvigorated the colonial spirit and began the movement for the preservation of America's past.

The colonial spirit and the poem's popularity brought many new visitors, but this did not translate into immediate business success for the inn. These new tourists were only paying a token amount for a brief, unscheduled house tour, and the inn was not being operated to capitalize on this fame. As late as 1892, we hear from one of the tenants, Lizzie Seymour, "Them poets and fellers havin' once bin in the house don't help to keep the wind out in the winter nor buy beef for the family."[6] The rebirth of the inn did not come until 1897. It took a new owner with capital resources and an artistic vision (who fortunately loved Longfellow) to bring it back to life.

From the colonial period through to today, it has been one long, continuous and connected story. Even as a farmhouse, it was still an object of interest to visitors. The inn has always had some life to it.

ERAS OF THE WAYSIDE INN

The best way to look at the inn over time is to separate the various eras by landlord tenure. We see:

The two generations of founding Hows and the beginning of the innkeeper tradition (although not at the Wayside Inn):

JOHN (1661–1680, his own tavern), the first in neighboring Marlborough, and the first How family tavern.
SAMUEL (1692–1710, his own tavern), he gave the land to David and likely helped build the inn.

The four generations of the How(e) family operating an evolving active inn through the colonial times (1702–1861, 159 years). These are <u>deed transfer dates</u>:

David (1702–1744, 41.7 years, a tavern from 1716 to 1744, 27.5 years)
Ezekiel (1744–1795, 51.2 years)
Adam (1795–1840, 45.8 years)
Lyman (1840–1861, 20.3 years)

A period of **Howe aunt and cousin ownership** and the Longfellow impact (auctioning some of the estate, subletting property, 1861–1893, 31.8 years).

A brief transition period of **local ownership** wanting to preserve the inn (1893–1897, 4.0 years).

Edward R. and Cora Lemon's restoration as an inn (1897–1923, 26.6 years).

Henry Ford's ownership, further restoration and asset accumulation/consolidation (1923–1945, 22.3 years).

The transition to a **historic trust, part I**: selling of assets and the 1955 fire/restoration period (1945–1959, 13.3 years).

The **modern-day ownership period, part II**: turning the inn into a sustainable business (1959–1989, the trust hired Francis [Frank] Koppeis to run it for 30.8 years).

And the current **modern-day ownership period, part III**: including the long-term strategic plan, bringing in new innkeepers, renovations and improvements to the business (1989–present, 21.7 years and counting).

From 1702 to the current day, the site has been occupied for 309 years. A tavern has stood on it for 295 years, and it has operated as such for 259 of these years.

Our story starts with the immigrant forefather, John How, and the settling of Sudbury.

John and Samuel How,

1630–1702

The First Settler, His Son and Their Taverns

Being thus passed the vast ocean and a sea of troubles before their preparation…they had now no friends to welcome them, nor inns to entertain and refresh their weatherbeaten bodies, no houses or much less towns to repair to…Besides, what could they see but a hideous and desolate wilderness full of wild beasts and wild men.
—*William Bradford, 1648*[7]

The unimaginable hardships our Pilgrim forefathers faced that first winter of 1620 did not stop the mass immigration destined to follow. Salem (1626) and thirty-five other Massachusetts settlements were established within the first ten years. Most were small, but everything changed when a royal charter for the Massachusetts Bay Colony was obtained in March 1629 by a small group of investors. The security needed to sponsor larger expeditions was now in place. Francis Higginson received funding to lead a group of three hundred settlers on five ships from England to Salem in May 1629. The next year, the famous "Winthrop Fleet" of eleven ships and seven hundred passengers set sail. Landing in Salem, its immigrants migrated out to Boston (incorporated in 1630) and the surrounding area. From 1630 to 1640, a time period known as the Great Migration, twenty thousand new immigrants, mainly Puritans, came to the colonial territory of Massachusetts. Religious freedom, economic hope, liberty and justice and property rights—which all free men sought—pushed these immigrants to look for a better life in all directions.

Just west of Boston, up the Charles River, Watertown (incorporated in 1630) was one of the first communities to start experiencing growing pains. By 1637, it was proposed that a company should push farther west from Watertown, "owning," as the grant application states, "to the straightness of accommodation

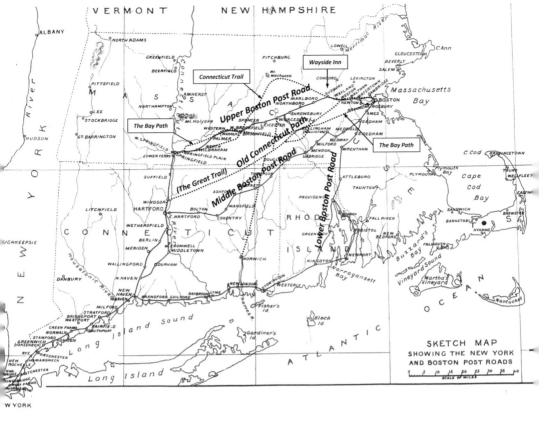

A map showing the routes of the old Boston Post Roads with added labeling and trail location notes by author. The Connecticut Path is ancient and much older than the Post Roads and Bay Path (see note 9). The Bay Path was laid out on top of a network of Indian trails in 1673 by government decree in an effort to make travel more efficient for the colonies. *Bay Path information is from Levi Badger Chase,* The Bay Path and Along the Way *(1914). Map of the various alignments of the Boston Post Road is from S. Jenkins,* The Old Boston Post Road *(New York: G.P. Putnam and Sons, 1914).*

and want of more meadow."[8] Not surprisingly, the earliest settlers had taken the choicest lots, and good land was getting scarce. How much property one had was important to his status, voting rights and such things as how many cows he could put on the public common. To get any land, one had to go where claims had yet to be made. In 1638, with land grants in hand, a group of fifty-four strong men and their families pushed twenty miles west into the wilderness to settle one of Massachusetts's first non-coastal towns: Sudbury.

Their route was likely already marked out for them, as Indian paths ran throughout the area. Earlier, in 1633, John Oldham and ten men had taken the ancient Indian trail known as the Old Connecticut Path (or "Great Trail," as it was otherwise known) to settle Wethersfield, Connecticut. In 1636, the Reverends Thomas Hooker and Samuel Stone, along with one hundred of their congregation and 160 cattle, followed this same route to settle Hartford.

This likely trampled the path nicely for the Sudbury settlers. Eight miles west of Watertown, between present-day Weston and Wayland (then part of Sudbury), the trail forked, and it is thought that the settlers picked up another Indian path known as the Connecticut Trail, going west off the Old Connecticut Path (the Old Connecticut Path continued south, now Route 126). The Connecticut Trail headed west through the area to become Sudbury Center, then up to Stowe, Lancaster, Princeton, West Brookfield and all the way out to the Connecticut River Valley.[9] Eventually, the Boston Post Road would be laid out over parts of these and other trails and would become the main road and mail route west to Albany (now Route 20).

Sudbury Settlement

The Sudbury settlers, either coming directly from England aboard the ship *Confidence* in 1638 or from towns east, had the names of Hayne, Rice, Noyes, Bent, Rutter, Goodenow, Stone, Maynard, Parmenter, Treadway, Pelham, (Pastor) Browne and How, among others. Because of the expected hardships, only strong and able men and women were granted land and encouraged to be the first settlers. The first death was not recorded until after the second year—an indication of their hardiness and ability to weather the wilderness better than most.

Sudbury (named after Pastor Browne's home village in England), was heavily timbered with chestnut, elm, oak and pine trees. Water resources were available, and wild game and fish were plentiful. The Nipmuck (or Nipnet) and Massachusetts Indians had settled this area long ago, calling it (and the river) *Musketaquid*, meaning "grassy banks." These natives had already cleared the land they needed for planting and game runs. Unfortunately, as a result of contact with European explorers, fur traders and fishermen, the northeast Indian ranks were decimated by the multiple plagues that hit their communities from 1616 to the 1630s. The winter of 1633 brought an especially hard smallpox outbreak amongst the local Musketaquid Indian population, and hundreds died. The surviving Indians were not hostile and sought opportunities for trade and protection.

Near what was to become the Wayside Inn was an important high point: Mount Nobscot (shortened by colonists from the native *Penobscot*, meaning "at the fall of the rocks"). This was the site of countless Indian camps over the past few centuries; their planting fields were at the foot of both the west and east sides of the hill. Identifiable native grinding stones, charred rocks from eons of fires and old paths are lasting vestiges of their existence.

For many years, a stone cairn existed on the summit of Nobscot. This was used by the Indians as a viewing platform where once eight native villages could be spotted. Nobscot was also home to Tantamous (aka Old Jethro), the famous (and later persecuted) Indian leader whose son was one of the fourteen natives to deed the Wayside Inn land to settlers in 1684.[10]

The original Sudbury settlement was established on the east side of the Sudbury River along the main Indian trail. Here the settlers worked the land

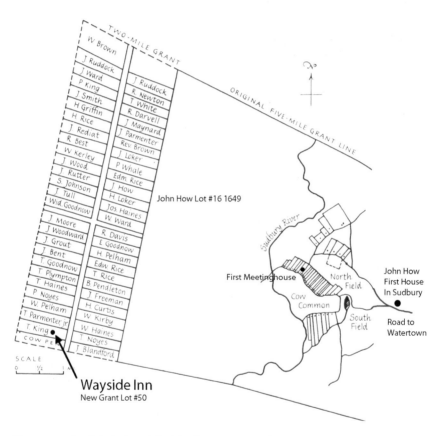

The area to the right is the original Sudbury on the east side of the Sudbury River (the rectangles are house lots; you also see the first millpond). This area was to split off and become the town of East Sudbury in 1780 (and was later incorporated as the town of Wayland in 1835). John How's house lot is identified in Hudson's *History of Sudbury*. Hudson states that John had one of the in-town lots but sold it to get the site marked. The "New Grant" was a two-mile extension to the western boundary of Sudbury granted by the general court in 1649 and confirmed in 1651. John How, Samuel's father, drew lot #16 (which he either sold or bequeathed to someone). The How Tavern/Wayside Inn land purchased from T. King(e) in 1676 is lot #50. Note that this map is not entirely to scale. *Map reproduced with permission from Wesleyan University Press, originally from* The Puritan Village *by Sumner Chilton Powell. Labels and additional edits by author.*

granted to them and built a community. A mill was established, and in 1643, the first meetinghouse was built.

John How (1602–1680 generally recorded), one of these first settlers, was, according to family tradition, the son of John How, Esquire, of Warwickshire, England. It is not clear when John came to the New World; he was not on the ship's register of the *Confidence*, he does not appear in Hotten's list of emigrants from 1600 to 1700 and early records from Watertown do not mention his name. Nevertheless, John was among the first men from Watertown to be given property title and to head out into this wilderness. John helped clear the land and worked with neighbors to build the new homes, garrisons, barns and bridges of this nascent town. He had become free of debt and any other legal restraints/indenturements by May 1640 and was admitted as a "freeman" to the Massachusetts Bay Colony (akin to being a full citizen). John was elected selectmen in 1642, and records show that he was one of six men contracted to build the meetinghouse.

Land disputes between the early settlers and the newer ones started pulling apart the community. (It was an issue of fairness, and John sided with the newer settlers. This was a complicated affair and is fully detailed in other texts.)[11] In 1656, John, together with twelve other Sudbury men, appealed to the general court for more land:

> *God hath beene pleased to increase our children, which are now diverse of them grown to man's estate; and wee, many of us, grown into years, so that wee should bee glad to see them settled before the Lord take us away from hence, as also God having given us some considerable quantity of cattle, so that wee are so straightened that we cannot so comfortably subsist as could be desired and some of us having taken some pains to view the country; wee have found a place which lyeth westward about eight miles from Sudbury which wee conceive might be comfortable for our subsistence.*[12]

MARLBOROUGH SETTLEMENT

The court granted land to these men eight miles west of Sudbury in an area later to become the colonial town of Marlborough. When they arrived, according to Marlborough's published history, they found the same decimated ranks of Native Americans as they did in Musketaquid. This small population was living in the area known as their "planting field," and they referred to their land as *Whipsuppenike* (or *Whipsufferadge*, said to mean "the place of sudden death"). Charles Hudson tells us in his 1862 *History of the Town of Marlborough*

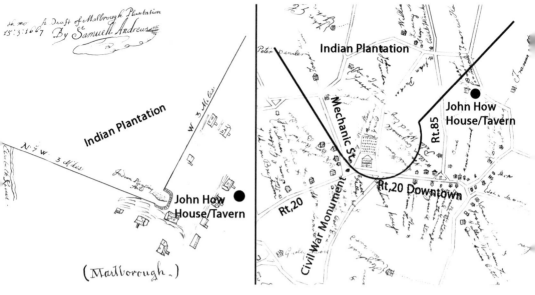

The map to the left is excerpted from one of the original maps of Marlborough, dated 1667, showing the town borders (not roads) and houses roughly in relationship to the Native American settlement. It shows the Indian planting field (the rounded section of the line, where the meeting house "mistakenly" was built on native property, causing strong resentment), as well as John How's tavern (said to be located at the intersection of two Indian paths). The map on the right is from 1803. Superimposing the 1667 boundaries (a rough approximation) and adding labels for the present-day main roads and the war monument, you can see where the early Native American and English settlements were with respect to the modern town. *Thanks to Bob Kane of the Marlborough Historical Society for help in connecting the two. Maps used with their permission.*

that the Indian planting field was "some one hundred and fifty acres located on the Hill back of the Common," and it was "more or less cultivated." (This is inside the round loop on map.) The land known as the Indian Plantation "extended north and east about three miles, and contained six thousand acres, the most of which was wild and uncultivated."

Hudson also tells us:

> *It seems, however, to be conceded, that John Howe was the first white inhabitant who settled in the town. He probably came to the place as early as 1657 or '58, and built him a cabin a little east of the Indian planting field, about one-third of a mile north-easterly of Spring Hill Meeting-House...Though his habitation was in the immediate vicinity of the native tribe of Indians, he succeeded in securing not only their friendship, but their entire confidence and esteem.*

John's friendship with the natives is highlighted through an often-told legend. John was asked to decide a dispute amongst two natives, one who planted a pumpkin vine on his land and the other whose land it was that the vine grew on and bore a pumpkin. The question of ownership was referred to John, whereupon he took a knife and cut the pumpkin in half, satisfying both parties.

John's trade is unknown.[13] For all his work in the wilderness, John probably had a fair amount of carpentry skills. John was busy building his second house, raising and protecting a family, farming and performing his civic and militia duties. Soon after the town was established, he became one of its first selectmen. Most notably, on October 1, 1661, at age fifty-nine, John was granted a license for keeping an ordinary, a privilege granted only to the most highly respected citizens.

These houses of public entertainment were first called either public houses (later, pubs), victualing houses, licensed houses or ordinaries. By the 1700s, they were called taverns or, in some cases, inns. The name tavern was usually given in New England and New York; in Pennsylvania, inn was more common. Both tavern and inn denoted a place for the full entertainment of travelers (man and beast)—entertainment meaning food and liquor served, animals cared for and a bed offered to sleep in. Sometimes, these places even cared for the poor.[14] In England, tavern meant a place only serving liquor and possibly food, but in the countryside of America, this was generally not the case.

Vestiges of John's house in Marlborough still remain at 29 Fowler Street, although it is not clear what, if anything, is original.[15] The 1929 *Howe Genealogies* states: "The old house has long since disappeared, but some of the chestnut cross beams used in it, were afterwards used, and so long preserved, in another building." The original house was to become Marlborough's first tavern, and John was to be the first of six generations of How innkeepers.

There are a handful of reminiscences stating that this tavern was known as the Black Horse Tavern. Others state that the John Jr. tavern (mentioned on the next page) was the Black Horse. There is a possibility that they were both called this, but perhaps at different times. Reliable primary source information that specifically states which

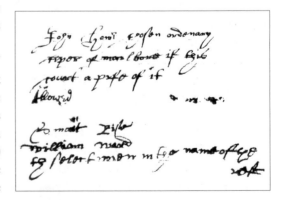

John How's original 1661 license petition preserved in the State Judicial Archives (Middlesex Portfolio, vol. 1, p. 236). "Ordinary," "Marlboro" and "William Ward" (a selectman at the time) can barely be discerned.

one—if either—was actually called the Black Horse has not been found after an exhaustive search.

John and his wife, Mary, had eleven children. Their oldest, John Jr. (1640–1676),[16] built a house with his wife, Elizabeth Ward, on the north side of Boston Post Road (across from Indianhead Hill [the current Home Depot plaza]), roughly two miles west of the Wayside Inn. John Jr. died at the age of thirty-five during an Indian attack near Sudbury on or about April 21, 1676 (possibly at the Sudbury fight against King Philip's braves, but it is not certain), and Indians destroyed his house. At some point his house became a tavern, but it is not clear when. If it was after John was killed, then likely it was John III (b. 1671) or his son John IV (b. 1697) who built it. John IV's son Cyprien (b. 1726, John Sr.'s great-great-grandson) eventually came to run it. Cyprien was also a captain of a company that marched to Cambridge on April 19, 1775, and he continued in the service during the war. By 1788, this tavern was called the Munroe-Wilson Place. By 1888, it was said that "there have been no buildings on this place for several years."[17]

John Sr. led an extraordinary life, finally succumbing to old age and the hardships of frontier living in 1680. Another of his sons, Colonel Thomas How (1656-1733), described as a courageous Indian fighter, inherited his father's house. He kept a tavern, likely here at this house, but it is unclear who ran it, as John How's widow, Mary, applied for a license renewal in 1681. If Thomas did carry on the business and farm, then the property appears to have passed eventually, by way of his son and grandson (both named Thomas), to Francis Howe (1750–1833). The How dwelling marked on the 1803 map shows Francis's name, but it does not say it is a tavern. It likely ceased operations by this time.

Thomas How's bond to run a public house in 1696 is interesting to read, as it illustrates the mores of this late Puritan society:

He shall not suffer or have any playing at cards, dice, tally, bowls, nine pins, billiards or any other unlawful game or games in his said house, or yard, or gardens, or backside, nor shall suffer to remain in his house any person or persons, not being his own family, on Saturday night, after dark, or on the Sabbath days, or during the time of God's Public Worship; nor shall he entertain as lodgers in his house any strangers, men or women, above the space of 48 hours, but such whose names and surnames he shall deliver to someone of the selectmen or constable of the town, unless they shall be such as he very well knoweth, and will ensure for his or their forth coming; nor shall sell any wine to the Indians or Negroes, nor suffer any children or servant or other person to remain in his house, tippling or drinking after 9 O'clock in the night; nor shall buy or take to preserve any stolen goods, nor willingly nor knowingly harbor in his house, barn, stable or otherwhere, any rogues, vagabonds, thieves, sturdy beggars, masterless men or women, or other notorious offenders whatsoever…nor shall any person or persons whatsoever sell or utter any wine, beer, ale, cider, rum, brandy or other liquors by defaulting, or by color of his license…nor shall entertain any person or persons to whom he shall be prohibited by law, or by any one of the Magistrates of the County, as persons of jolly conversation or given to tippling.[18]

In addition to these two known How Taverns in Marlborough from this side of the family (John/Thomas's and John Jr.'s), there was another early How Tavern established by one Abraham How(e). Abraham was an early settler but was said to be unrelated to John.[19] With at least three How Taverns in Marlborough, it is obvious why the How Tavern *of Sudbury* would be so described. Another famous tavern in Marlborough, though not part of this story, is the circa 1665 Williams Tavern across town from John How, near Williams Pond on the Post Road. It was once the most significant tavern in Marlborough, and George Washington stopped to dine there in 1789. This tavern unfortunately was bulldozed in the late 1940s.

John's second oldest son, Samuel (1642–1713), had moved back from Marlborough to Sudbury long before his father died. Samuel becomes the thread in this story. After his marriage in 1663 to Martha Bent, daughter of one of John Sr.'s oldest friends from Sudbury, he was deeded forty-four acres of land in Sudbury by his wife's family. This was in the Lanham section of town, roughly six miles southeast of the Wayside Inn property. Samuel and Martha had seven children. After Martha died, Samuel married Sarah Clapp in 1685 and had six more children.

The 1929 *Howe Genealogies* tells us that, like his father before him, Samuel was a man of great energy and public spirit. He was a carpenter, and records show that he built the town pound, the cart bridge near his home (on which he collected a toll) and stocks in front of the meetinghouse. He was a juryman, selectman, assessor, surveyor, constable and land speculator (amassing lands all the way down to Lake Cochituate, which was the subject of a dispute by the Natick Indians). He served in King Philip's War (in Captain Nathan Davenport's company) and later was an officer in the militia. Also, like his father before him, he became an innkeeper. When Samuel was fifty years old, the court granted him a license to run a house of public entertainment. In a communication on July 29, 1692, by Joseph Noyes, one of the selectmen of Sudbury, to the Middlesex County Court, Noyes says of Samuel:

It has been in the minds of most of us that there should be none to retail drink amongst us by reason of the growing of the sin of drunkenness amongst us. Our fathers came into this wilderness to enjoy the gospel and his ordinances in its purity and the conversion of heathen but instead of converting them, amongst other sins we have taught them to be drunkards which we may have cause to fear God has permitted them to be such a scourge as at this present.

There be those that desire licenses but such as cannot command themselves are not fit for such an important trust. All things considered it is not mine one mind only but of some others that Col. Samuel How is best accommodated and the most suitable man that presents himself willing to undertake to entertain travelers which as far as I understand is the only or least the chief end of a house of entertainment and not town drunkards.[20]

Samuel's last license petition for innkeeping, found in the State Judicial Archives, was issued in 1710. His son Elisha was issued a license to sell "strong drink" on June 24, 1711,[21] presumably taking over his father's business.

In addition to becoming an innkeeper, Samuel did something else noteworthy—on June 5, 1676, he purchased the "Squadron Four New Grant Lot #50" from the heirs of Thomas King(e).[22] This property was the acreage on which the Wayside Inn was to eventually be built. There has been a little controversy over the property, as many turn-of-the-century magazine articles and book references place Samuel's tavern on this land. There is no proof that Samuel lived anywhere else in Sudbury except in the Lanham area house near his toll bridge. Nearby, there was a gristmill in which Samuel had a 25 percent share. His house, like his brother's, was burned by King Philip's braves in 1676. Samuel likely rebuilt on this site, but history is not entirely clear on this point. There is no trace left of his old house; new homes occupy the presumed site. Interestingly, the remains of a much-later-reconstructed old stone cart bridge near the site of Samuel's lot still cross over the Sudbury River just north of Potter Street in Framingham (which was then Sudbury).

Of Samuel's thirteen children,[23] his sixth oldest child was David, and David is the next thread in the How Tavern/Wayside Inn story.

HOW FAMILY

Built first tavern in Marlborough

John How
Innkeeper
b. 1620
m. Mary [Jones] (no date)
d. 1680

Great-Great-Great-Grandfather
Children
1. John b. 1640
2. Samuel b. 1642
3. Isaac b. 1648
4. Josiah b. 1650
5. Thomas b. 1656
6. Eleazer b. 1662

Built tavern in Lanham area (then Sudbury)

Samuel How
Innkeeper
b. Oct 20, 1642
m. Martha Bent, 1663
m. Sarah Clapp, 1685
d. April 13, 1716

Great-Great-Grandfather
Children
1. John b. 1664
2. Mary b. 1665
3. Samuel b. 1668
4. Martha b. 1669
5. Daniel b. 1672 d. 1680
6. David b. 1674
7. Hannah b. 1677
8. Elisha (no date)
9. Daniel b. 1690
10. Nehemiah b. 1693
11. Moses b. 1695
12. Ebenezer b. 1697
13. Micaiah b. 1700

Built tavern to become the Wayuck inn

David How
Innkeeper
b. Nov 2, 1674
m. Hepzibah Death, 1700
d. April 15, 1769

Great-Grandfather to Lyman
Children
1. Thankful b. 1703
2. Hepsibah b. 1706
3. Eliphalet b. 1710
4. Israel b. 1712
5. Ruth b. 1715
6. David b. 1717
7. Ezekiel b. 1720

Ezekiel How
Innkeeper
b. April 5, 1720
m. Bathsheba Stone, 1743
m. Rebecca Ruggles, 1772
d. Oct 15, 1796

Grandfather to Lyman
Children
1. Ruth b. 1745
2. Ann b. 1746-7
3. Hepzibah b.1749
4. Bathsheba b. 1752
5. Ezekiel b. 1756
6. Olive b. 1758
7. Eliphalet b. 1761
8. Adam(s) b. 1763
9. Jane (no date)

Adam Howe
Innkeeper
b. May 15, 1763
m. Jeruha Balcom, 1795
d. Dec 10, 1840

Father to Lyman
Children
1. Jerusha b. 1797
2. Rebecca b. 1799, d. 1803
3. Lyman b. 1801
4. Winthrop b. 1804, d. 1806
5. Adam b. 1805
6. Abiel Whinthrop b. 1807

Lyman Howe
Innkeeper
b. Nov 6, 1801
d. April 1861

Children

DAVID HOW, 1702–1746

The Builder of the Tavern and the First Landlord

The gods who are most interested in the human race preside over the tavern…The tavern will compare favorably with the church. The church is the place where prayers and sermons are delivered, but the tavern is where they are to take effect, and if the former are good, the latter cannot be bad.
—Henry David Thoreau

David How (1674–1759), son of Samuel, married Hepzibah Death on December 25, 1700, and needed a home for his family. On June 4, 1702, Samuel deeded David lot #50, where the inn was to be built. The actual deed provides additional evidence that David, not Samuel, built the first tavern here. It states that Samuel gave David "a certain parcel of land and meadows containing by estimation one hundred and thirty acres." If Samuel had his tavern on this lot, it clearly would have specified a dwelling. There also exists in the archives a letter dated 1951 by Frank H. Noyes, a Boston attorney, who investigated this at length. He writes, "When one has read, as I have, all the recorded deeds to and from Samuel…I am confident that when Samuel conveyed to his son David this 130 acres of New Grant land, there were no buildings upon it."

Samuel held this property for twenty-six years prior to giving it to David. It seems likely he traveled to it a few times and possibly started planning for its later use. We can just imagine Samuel and/or David following the old Indian trail leading to this area and picking a spot in a protected valley with a brook and nearby waterfall. It is thought that David began immediately to construct his new house (later to become

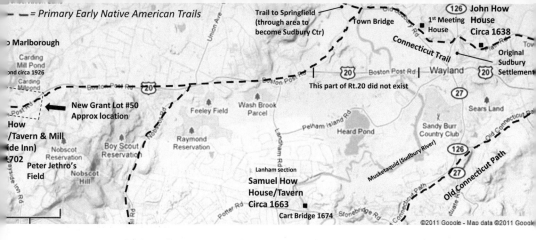

A properly scaled map showing the original Sudbury settlement, some of the Indian trails, Samuel's cart bridge, Mount Nobscot and the location of the Wayside Inn. Samuel's Tavern was about six miles from lot #50.

the Wayside Inn) once the land passed to him. His father, Samuel, was a carpenter and likely helped with the construction (he was about sixty at the time; he would pass away at age of seventy-one in 1713). The first written record crudely referencing a homestead on this site is a map dated 1707.[24] It is suspected that the house was built in 1702–3. David would dam the waterfall sometime around 1727 and build a mill.[25]

The First House, Later to Become the First Tavern

The original structure was thought to be two stories and included the front door and the two windows to the right of the current building (the Bar Room). Some architectural evidence of this was found during the 1956–58 reconstruction—researchers found equally spaced mortises in the beam over the fireplace (indicating that it was an outside wall), nail holes on the outside of the northeast corner post and clay from a hearth on an inside beam.[26] One of the 1890-era tenants, Mr. Seymour, cites much earlier "brick being found in the north wall of the front rooms" and "beam placement" as indications that this might be the oldest part of the inn.

There is some speculative conflicting evidence, however. Samuel Bent's 1897 oration to the Society of Colonial Wars mentions what he heard from a previous owner: "[The original structure was] generally supposed to be the L in the rear of the present edifice, although others speak of some part of it as standing as late as 1829, implying the original structure has by this time disappeared." Joseph Seabury, a noted architectural

A conceptual drawing of David How's first house, early 1700s. *Drawn for the Wayside Inn by Eleanor Raymond.*

writer, wrote in the July 1914 *House Beautiful* magazine: "The east wing (to the right) is very old, and might well have formed an important part of the original." Both of these seem to point to the great age of the Old Kitchen wing, but there is not enough information to draw any further conclusions. The Bar Room progression seems more plausible.

As workmen built the structure with David, legend has it that they spent the nights at the Parmenter Garrison, a few hundred yards to the east, to protect themselves from Indian attacks. (A stone marker commemorates the site of this garrison.) Even though King Philip's War ended in 1676, this continued to be a dangerous period. Local Indian attacks still occurred and were recorded in the 1690s, in 1704 and in 1705. In 1707, there was a noted Indian attack in nearby Marlborough, now within the bounds of Northborough, where young Mary Goodenow was slain. Colonel Thomas How, David's uncle, the "Indian fighter," led the militia to capture and kill most of this group of marauding natives. His petition for a bounty is in the state archives. Lovewell's War on the colonial frontier also continued from 1722 to 1725, drawing troops and keeping people alert. In addition to Indians, bears and wolves were also a problem. Barricades and fences had to be constructed around the building for added protection.

By 1716, David and Hepzibah had four of their seven children. They needed more room, not only for their growing family but also for a new desire: the accommodation of travelers. It is thought that they expanded the house to include the front (current) parlor section and chamber room above it (the two windows to the left of the front door); however, there is no definitive record of any of the expansions from the small house to the current gambrel house.

There is a record of the petition sent in that year on their behalf:[27]

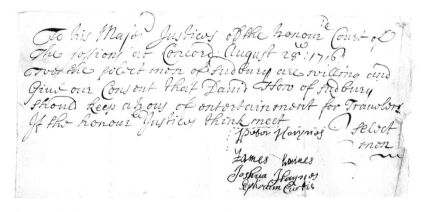

The original 1716 selectmen's approval and petition to the higher court for David to open a "hous of entertainment for travelers."

To his Majies Justices of the honourd Court of sessions at Concord August 28th, 1716, We the selectmen of Sudbury are willing and give our Consent that David How of Sudbury should keep a hous of entertainment for Travelers if the honourd Justices think meet

Peter Haynes Joshua Haynes

James Haynes Ephraim Curtis

Selectmen

This was David's application for a license to keep a house of public entertainment, which was approved. The first known reference to this How Tavern comes from Judge Samuel Sewell's well-known travel journals (Judge Sewell was famous for his involvement in the Salem witch trials). On April 27, 1716, he traveled from Watertown to Worcester. He writes, "Got to How's about one-half hour by the sun." (The Massachusetts Historical Society [MHS] notes this as the How Tavern at the Wayside Inn location, not the Samuel How one in Lanham.)[28] Assuming the MHS is correct, since David's first license was requested in *August* 1716, it seems it was operating as some type of rest stop prior to getting its full license. Though the evidence is very thin and this business was highly regulated, there does remain a very remote possibility that Samuel was somehow involved in the business early on (before 1713).

David's remote location on the main road to Marlborough and points west probably made it an ideal stop for travelers. Like Judge Sewell, people were likely stopping there already. Growing up in a tavern, David had the skills to run this type of business profitably, so it made sense to pursue a license, especially since he was bound by strict colonial laws requiring a license for this type of activity.

An ongoing civic matter in town may also have pushed David to pursue a license. The established meetinghouse was all the way across the river in what is now Wayland. Every Sabbath day, it was a requirement to journey there to attend service. In colonial days, taverns were usually located near meetinghouses so that weary worshippers, chilled during the long winter services and the ride out to them, could get some refreshment, warmth and an opportunity to socialize. Perhaps it was thought that if a tavern were built on the west side, a meetinghouse would soon follow. Petitions (which David signed) to the general court to establish a meetinghouse and separate township on the west side started in 1707 and came up again in 1714. By 1722, it was agreed that a new "precinct" could be formed on the west side with its own meetinghouse. This second meetinghouse was built in 1723 where the First Parish Church now stands in Sudbury Center, a bit far from David. (Interestingly, approval to split off the town finally came later in 1780, this time through a petition by the east side residents who thought they were getting unfairly taxed. Most of the people were living on the west side, but most of the wealth was on the east side. They gave up the original town name—Sudbury—to get this tax relief.) It is not entirely clear what the social-political landscape was like in the early days of the town's expansion west, but it seems David was not happy with some of the developments. By 1740, David had led another petition to the court for a new town to be carved out in the How Tavern area. This was never approved. David was elected a town selectman in 1741, possibly to appease him and end the petitions.

EZEKIEL HOW, 1746–1796

Revolutionary-Era Landlord and the Growing Inn

> *Whoe'er has travell'd life's dull round*
> *Where'er his stages may have been,*
> *May sigh to think he still has found*
> *The warmest welcome at an inn.*
> —*Shenstone, written on a window of an inn*

The growing mail and travel business on the Post Road kept the tavern busy. With the inn prospering and David's family increasing in size, a larger house was probably needed. It is assumed that when Ezekiel (1720–1796), David's youngest child, married Bathsheba Stone in 1743 and resided at the inn, Ezekiel and his father began enlarging the four-room house to one of more spacious proportions. Ezekiel and Bathsheba had ten children.

Ezekiel How was deeded the property on February 5, 1744.[29] His innkeeper term has traditionally been designated as being from 1746 to 1796 because of an old sign found at the inn back in the mid- to late 1800s. This sign

This silhouette of Ezekiel How was hanging in the inn's Parlor in 1931. Its authenticity cannot be confirmed. *Used with permission of the Sudbury Historical Society.*[30]

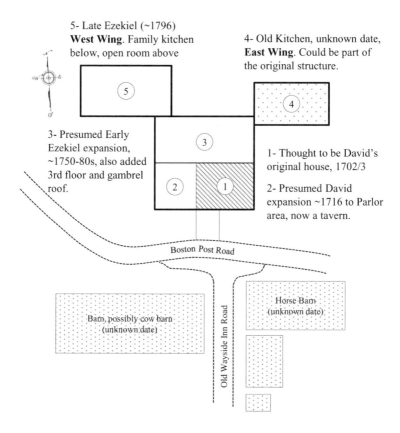

5- Late Ezekiel (~1796) **West Wing**. Family kitchen below, open room above

4- Old Kitchen, unknown date, **East Wing**. Could be part of the original structure.

3- Presumed Early Ezekiel expansion, ~1750-80s, also added 3rd floor and gambrel roof.

1- Thought to be David's original house, 1702/3

2- Presumed David expansion ~1716 to Parlor area, now a tavern.

Boston Post Road

Old Wayside Inn Road

Barn, possibly cow barn (unknown date)

Horse Barn (unknown date)

The generally presumed expansion of the house. Few records exist on any How-period house construction.

was mentioned in an August 10, 1868 *Boston Journal* article and was also illustrated in Drake's 1874 book. To add further confusion to this, Ezekiel's first innkeeper's license is dated from 1748 (and David's last was 1747).[31] At the same time that Ezekiel was deeded the inn, his brother David Jr. was deeded half of the adjacent Hop Brook mill property. David Sr. lived until 1759 (the age of eighty-five) and undoubtedly assisted with both businesses.

The expansion of the inn to the current gambrel-roofed structure is attributed to Ezekiel's period. No specific records exist of this work, but Ezekiel's will mentions a "new kitchen" (the west wing). Since this was an ell, it must have been added to some larger house, so it is assumed the main house was expanded sometime in the David-Ezekiel period. The barns across the street were also likely built or expanded at this time. There exists

How Tavern looking east, undated (likely early 1860s). It shows the elm tree and its knotty roots, a favorite place for sitting. The tree likely held the inn's first signboard. This is one of four very early pictures in the archives. The tavern probably looked something like this late in Ezekiel's era, although it is not clear how the west wing fully developed.

one commentary on the roofline of the old house. Seabury tells us in his *House Beautiful* article: "Though historians differ in describing the original size and character of the building, we are told that a great lean-to roof swept from the ridge-pole nearly to the ground in the rear, while the front portion doubtless took the shape of the usual gambrel roof."

THE GROWING BUSINESS

During Ezekiel's time, commerce was expanding, and traffic outside the tavern was now far more than just the solitary figure on horseback. More and more farmers and drovers were passing by as they brought their produce and herds to the Boston and Brighton markets. Large canvas-topped wagons were likely a frequent sight. In 1783, Captain Levi Pease of Shrewsbury, Massachusetts, inaugurated a successful stage line between Boston and Hartford, running right past the tavern. This was one of many coach services to pass this way.

The stagecoach business required some logistical efficiency to support, as the coach service had a schedule to maintain. A new routine around the tavern likely developed, much like that at other stops; when coaches approached, the driver would sound a horn announcing their imminent arrival. This was a signal for the innkeeper, housemaids and stable hands to be at the ready with food, refreshments and service for "man and beast." The horn of the approaching mail coach also routinely brought a crowd to the door to see what news and excitement it might carry.

Soldiers also passed by more frequently now. Their marches west and north to French and Indian War (1754–63) battles and garrison postings at Lake George, Ticonderoga, Crown Point (where 176 Sudbury men served on this expedition in 1756), Fort Edwards, Fort Number Four and Canada took them right by the tavern.

The Inn and the Revolution

Ezekiel was not only an innkeeper, but he was also a lieutenant colonel of the Fourth Regiment, Middlesex County Militia, under Colonel James Barrett of Concord. This was a time when tensions between England and the colonies were mounting, and the citizenry was preparing for the inevitable confrontation. There is a record of Ezekiel getting paid by the town for supplying arms to his company on October 3, 1774:

> *To Capt. Ezekiel How for 20 guns and Bayonets 27— 0—2*
> *600 pounds Lead 8—16—0*
> *300 french Flynts [9 or] 19— —11*
> *Chest for the arms and carting them 7—2—2*[32]

In March, they still did not seem fully prepared for the battle that would occur a month later. Lieutenant Colonel How penned this "return."[33]

> *March 27 1775*
> *The return of the Severall Companys of Militia and Minute in sd Town viz:*

Capt. Moses's Company—92 men of them, 18 no guns. at Least one third part ye forelocks un fit for Sarvis. Others wais un a quipt.

Capt. Aaron Hayns Company—60 Men weel provided with Arms for most of them Proveded with Bayonets or hatchets a boute one quarter part with Catrige Boxes.

Capt. Joseph Smith's Company consisting of...75 able Bodied men forty well a quipt twenty Promisto find and a quip themselves Emedetly fifteen no guns and other wais un a quipt.

The Troop Capt Isaac Locer (Loker)...21 Besides what are on the minit Role well a quipt.

Returned by
Ezekiel How. Lertn Conl.

When the Lexington alarm sounded on April 19, 1775, the first news of trouble came to Sudbury between three and four o'clock in the morning from a Concord express rider. Immediately, the church bell was rung, musketry discharged and the six companies (302 men) of the town mustered into service. Lieutenant Colonel How led two of these companies, and by nine o'clock all the men had reached Concord. Ezekiel's story is commonly told as follows (here by Bent):

When they came within sight of Colonel Barrett's house they halted, before them were the British, engaged in their mischievous work. Gun carriages had been collected and piled together to be burned (the cannon were buried and not found), and the residence of the colonel had been ransacked. They halted, and Lt. Col Howe exclaimed, "If any blood has been shed, not one of those rascals shall escape." Disguising himself, he rode on to ascertain the truth. This was around nine in the morning, which showed the celerity with which the Sudbury troops had moved...the Sudbury companies were but a short distance from the North Bridge when the first opposition was made to the haughty enemy...At any rate, the Sudbury companies then joined in the pursuit of the retreating British, and in at least two of the sharp encounters—Merriam's Corner and the other at Hardy's Hill, they bravely bore their part. They sustained a loss of two men killed and one wounded.

Also on that fateful Wednesday morning of April 19, 1775, 110 Worcester minutemen under Captain Timothy Bigelow stopped to rest at the tavern. They had just marched twenty-two miles from their homes and were

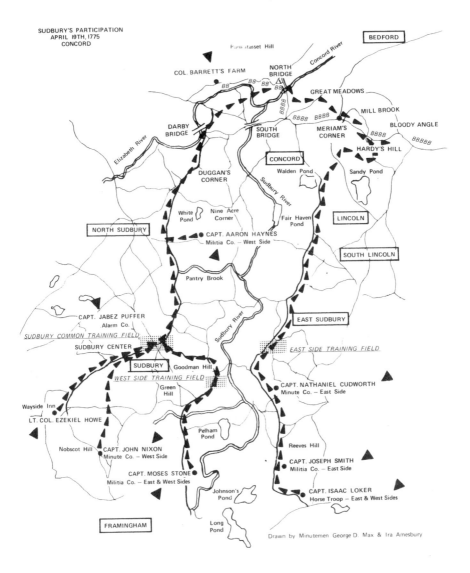

Routes taken by the various companies of the Sudbury Minute and Militia on April 19, 1775. *Used with permission of the Sudbury Historical Society.*

headed for Concord. When they heard Percy's cannons firing, they rousted themselves out the door and headed on a quick march to Lexington, another eighteen miles ahead.

Ezekiel's oldest son, Ezekiel How Jr., also participated in the skirmish that day. He ran the twelve miles to the bridge from his home. He passed the British soldier who was (mistakenly said to be) tomahawked in the head near the bridge, and he nearly passed out. He managed to push on, fighting the British as they retreated. The legend goes that later in the war, Lieutenant How was severely wounded at Saratoga. Fearing death, he bought a silver watch and made arrangements to send it home to his betrothed. He recovered, brought the watch home, married the girl and lived to old age. Strangely, his petition for a pension makes no mention of any injury.[34] The watch is currently on display at the inn. A hard-to-read inscription states: "Bought off an officer in Burgoyne's army at Saratoga for thirty silver dollars. The officer was at the time out of money, and sold it under price." Ezekiel Jr. built a house just south of the inn (on Wayside Inn Road, just over the Sudbury border in Framingham) that looks like a miniature version of the inn. Ezekiel How Jr.'s grave is thought to be on this property.[35]

The Sudbury Militia would go on to follow the British all the way back to Boston. Some returned in a few days; others came back after a month of providing some military duty. Three companies of Sudbury soldiers would participate in the Battle of Bunker Hill two months later. Ezekiel, with his commodity procurement skills, would serve a role supplying the troops around Boston until the British left in 1776. He was promoted to colonel by this time and then resigned in 1779 for reasons of "ill health" (he also likely saw his lucrative supply business drying up as the war moved south). He lived for seventeen more years.

Other Revolutionary War notables were said to have passed by or stopped at the inn. On July 2, 1775, George Washington passed the inn on his journey from Philadelphia to Cambridge to take command of the army. He left Brookfield on July 1 and traveled through Worcester, Marlborough and Sudbury on his way to Watertown, where he arrived early on the morning of July 2. That evening, Washington left for Cambridge. A monument was installed in 1914 outside the inn to commemorate that he "passed this place." Years later, on October 23, 1789, Washington rode past the inn again on his tour of New England. He had breakfast at the United States Arms Tavern in Worcester, dined at the Williams Tavern in Marlborough and lodged at the Flag Tavern in Weston. While he clearly passed by the inn, there is no mention of his stopping there. Whether he did or not is unknown.

Legend has it that in August 1824 (mentioned by Bent; some point to 1825), the famous Revolutionary War general the Marquis de Lafayette passed by or stayed at the inn (he was in the Boston area both years). This has often been disputed, as Lafayette kept meticulous records and never mentioned the inn. Newspapers also picked up his every move, and nothing has ever been found referencing a stay at the inn. Lafayette traveled between Boston and Worcester several times on later visits to the United States. The one day there is even a remote possibility that he was at the inn was on October 14, 1784, when he stayed "at some unnamed place between Worcester and Watertown."[36] Nevertheless, the room at the top right of the stairs has, for a very long time, been called the Lafayette Room, as this is where the great general and his valet were said to have stayed.

While the Revolution was a defining part of Ezekiel's era, there are a few other scattered pieces of information about his life and the inn during this time that can help form the picture of what it was like back in the late 1700s.

Food and Drink at the Early Tavern

Hudson tells us in his 1889 *History of Sudbury*:

> In all of these taverns strong drink was probably sold. Licenses were granted by the Provincial or Colonial Court, and the landlords were usually men of some prominence. Taverns were considered useful places in the early times, and laws existed relating to the rights of both landlord and guest. In the period of the Revolutionary War, when a price-list was determined at Sudbury for various common commodities, the following was established for taverns:
>
> 1779—*Mugg West India Phlip 15*
> *New England Do 12*
> *Toddy in proportion*
> *A Good Dinner 20*
> *Common Do 12*
> *Best Supper & Breakfast 15 Each*
> *Common Do 12, Lodging 4*

There is a receipt on display at the inn that shows between May 23, 1769, and July 23, 1770, upwards of 225 gallons of rum was bought by then Captain Ezekiel How from a Zachariah Johonnoh. Rum was likely a favored beverage at the time. The basement corner under the Parlor was called the rum cellar (and later the wine cellar).

While not contemporary, a newspaper article published on December 16, 1923, by the *Sunday Telegram* discusses early meals at the How Tavern:

The food, of course, was cooked before the huge open fireplaces…In 1713 wealthy people had Irish beef and strong butter, cheese, turkey, lamb, oysters, fish, and large lobsters at 3 half-pence each! Just ordinary people had salt pork, baked beans, fried eggs, and after 1740, boiled dinner with potatoes, which were scatteringly used in this country after 1720.

SLAVE OWNERSHIP

The Howe Papers in the archives mention two slaves being at the inn. In 1773, there was the "Sale of negro slave 'Portsmouth,'" signed by William Baldwin, to E. Howe. Later, in 1779: "Received of Colonel Ezekiel How 200 pounds on account of negro garll sold him in October." Portsmouth (said to be from Portsmouth, New Hampshire) is mentioned in several instances throughout the records. He was also called "Port" or "Ponto," he was thirty-three years old when he arrived and he was said to be a dwarf. He slept in a small bunk (or "shelf") in the attic. Portsmouth was very timid, and tradition states that he would hide under a low shelf in the hallway when strangers were present. Slavery was outlawed in Massachusetts in 1780. When Ezekiel gave Portsmouth his release, the oft-repeated story says that Port replied, "No Massa, you picked the meat, now you have to pick the bones." It is mentioned that he is buried somewhere on the property, but this cannot be confirmed.

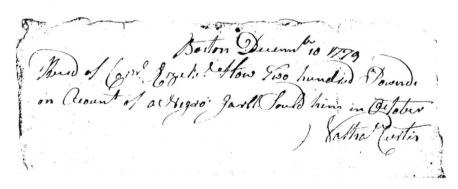

The 1779 receipt for Ezekiel How's payment of 200 pounds for a female slave.

The Red Horse Name and Signboard

Drake's sign in his 1874 *Historic Mansions and Fields of Middlesex* book, modified to show the correct 1716 date. Drake erroneously had the date 1686 on this sign, a date that has caused confusion for over one hundred years. Many scholars have researched this, and no one has ever been able to find anything linked to this date or the 1683 date that was painted on later signs. (The year 1676 was when Samuel acquired the property—David was two—and 1684 was when the Indian deed came through; those are the closest meaningful dates).

Legend has it that Ezekiel changed the name of the inn to the Red Horse Tavern about 1746. There is no documented evidence of this, and no records show that the Red Horse name was even used in the eighteenth century. Two early nineteenth-century recollections mention a *black* horse on the sign. One of them even states, "It was known to all the surrounding region as 'Adam How's Tavern.'"[37] Other documents simply refer to it as the How Tavern. Thoreau, on visiting the tavern on May 22, 1853, writes in his journal, "This is the third windy day following two days of rain...Left our horse at the How Tavern. The oldest date on the sign is 'D.H. 1716'... Went on to Nobscot." Longfellow similarly writes in 1862, "Drive with Fields to the old Howe Tavern in Sudbury." Ezekiel's will and inventory do not mention "red horse" anywhere (nor does his will even mention "tavern"). A reminiscence in the archives by a student writer named Florence Whittemore dated July 19, 1865, identifies the inn as the "Old Howe Tavern" and goes on to say that it is "the name which the house has always borne."

The Red Horse name does get some support. Adeline Lunt's September 1880 *Harper's New Monthly Magazine* article documenting visits there from the 1830s to the 1850s is titled "The Red Horse Tavern," so trusting her, there is at least some indication that the inn had "Red Horse" in its name back in the 1800s. Longfellow mentions that "the Red Horse prances on the sign" in 1862. There is also a *Boston Journal* newspaper article dated August 10, 1868, by a pen-named "Zed" stating that he saw a red horse on one side of a sign and initials on the other side. A Mrs. Seymour, "who used to play around the Wayside Inn in the days when Lyman Howe was Landlord," said she "remembers the original Red Horse sign, which in those days was hanging on the end of an old barn where the stage coaches were put up."[38] Atherton Rogers writes a recollection of the late 1800s and mentions that "the old Red Horse sign or what was left of it was still up when I was there."[39] While there is no evidence of the use of the Red Horse name in the eighteenth century, there is little doubt that the inn was called the Red Horse by the mid-nineteenth century. It should be pointed out that there is very little narrative at all on anything in the eighteenth century, so this lack of evidence does not necessarily refute the legend.

Building the West Wing

The inn has in its possession an itemized bill dated 1785 that suggests some renovations took place. This bill was only for a limited amount of material, but among the items listed were white pine boards and "sash stuff." It is likely that there were many other bills, as it is believed that around this time Ezekiel built on the "new kitchen at the west end of my dwelling house with the lower room adjoining," as mentioned in his will.

Living Space

Ezekiel's will may also point to where his living space was in the inn. He bequeaths to his wife, Rebecca (this is his second wife, now of twenty-four years),

> *the improvement of the one half of my homestead farm…also the improvement of the new kitchen at the west end of my dwelling house with the lower room adjoining thereto* [likely the How Sitting Room] *with the cellar under the same, also the long chamber over the aforesaid room* [the ballroom before it was fitted out], *with the northwest bed chamber* [the Hobgoblin Room] *in the old part of said dwelling house with the one half of the garret in the west end of said house* [the attic above the Hobgoblin Room] *with the privilege of passing and repassing at all times.*

It seems Rebecca received the entire back, northwestern corner of the house. Quite possibly, the second-floor northwest bedchamber she got to keep was their old bedroom.

The long chamber mentioned would soon become the New Hall, as the Old Hall in the original gambrel building (the Hobgoblin Room) was just too small for dancing (or it was already a bedroom). Later, the New Hall would be called the 1800 Ballroom, as it was believed to have been fitted out fully by the early 1800s.

LAND ACQUISITIONS

Though the records by themselves do not tell the full story, it appears that Ezekiel or Ezekiel Jr. (or both) were amassing significant acreage. Sudbury town records show that an Ezekiel How was party to receiving at least seventeen deeds from other landholders from 1748 to 1789.[40] His final deed to his son Adam and his will show the family acreage had almost doubled to 240 acres.

EZEKIEL'S BROTHER, THE NEIGHBORING HOW ESTATE

Before parting from Ezekiel's tale, we should note the enterprise of Ezekiel's older brother David Jr. (b. 1717). Their father, David Sr., had dammed the Hop Brook and established a mill slightly upstream from where the present-day gristmill is located, possibly by the 1727 date mentioned. The 1744 deed mentions a "New Grist Mill," meaning 1744 was when the first mill was there (refuting the 1727 hypothesis) or implying that it was an addition or replacement. This deed gave half the mill to David Jr.; six years later, David Sr. sold him all of it.[41] A 1763 survey in the Sudbury town archives shows this mill listed as a corn mill. It stayed in this family for five generations, passing from David to David Jr. to his son Joseph, to his son Buckley, to his son Joseph Calvin (1817–1905). Joseph Calvin operated it as a shoe-nail and tack factory. The family homestead was across the street. Both the house and mill were quite significant structures; the How Tavern area must have been quite an impressive part of the Post Road to ride by in those early days.

END OF THE ERA

Colonel Ezekiel How lived to see the west side of Sudbury split off as a separate town in 1780 (he was involved in these negotiations). In October

Ezekiel How, 1746–1796

The original How mill site, photo from the mid-1800s. The mill buildings were located right on the dam. These buildings came down in the late 1920s when the new gristmill was built.

1796, at the age of seventy-seven, he passed away and was buried in the Revolutionary War Cemetery in Sudbury Center. He ran the inn for over fifty years, the longest of any landlord. In the inventory of his estate, there is the famous coat of arms, appraised at $4, his firearms at $8, his library at $10, the clock at $30, a silver tankard at $25, a plate at $30 and the homestead with 240 acres of land at $6,500, the entire appraisal amounting to $9,531 (a small fortune in today's dollars). He left most of his personal articles to his "well beloved granddaughter, Hepzibah Brown" and the residual of his estate, "after many legacies," to his third son, Adam.

ADAM HOWE, 1796–1840

*The Third How(e) Tavern Landlord
and the Prosperous Years*

*There is no private house in which people can enjoy themselves so well as at a capital
tavern….No, Sir; there is nothing which has yet been contrived by man by which so much
happiness is produced as by a good tavern or inn.*
—Dr. Samuel Johnson, March 1776

On March 24, 1795, a little over a year and a half before he was to
pass away, Ezekiel deeded the homestead property to his youngest son,
Adam. "Uncle Adam" (1763–1840), as he was familiarly known, is described
in a letter to the *Boston Journal* dated August 13, 1868: "Briskly did he move
about in his long blue frock of wool, regardless of the style of his guests,
while his good spouse (Jerusha Balcom) in plain calico gown presided with
earnest zeal over the details of the house."

These were the heydays of the inn. Horse travel along the Post Road
required frequent stops, and the old pump in front of the inn became a
welcome respite. The country was moving away from the war years into an
age of discovery and exploration. Two reminiscences paint a small picture
of what it was like during Adam's tenure.

THE INN DURING ADAM'S TIME

Adeline Lunt, in the September 1880 *Harper's New Monthly Magazine*,
describes Adam as "painstaking and prosperous. His broad acres," she

Adam Howe, 1796–1840

Hand-inked drawings obtained by the archives in 1958 and said to be Adam and Jerusha Howe. They cannot be authenticated.[42]

says, "stretched through meadow and woodland for miles away. His good wife, with ample force of male and female accessory, conducted the ménage, and their two sons, Lyman and Adam, and one daughter Jerusha, made up the perfect family picture." Adam and Jerusha had six children; two died young (Winthrop and Rebecca), and their youngest, Abiel Winthrop, was born in 1807, but little else is known about him (he may have passed away in 1845).

Lydia M. Childs, the famous writer and abolitionist, penned a recollection of what the inn was like in 1828 (this is the earliest recollection of the inn on record, though it was written forty-four years later). She writes in the 1872 *National Standard Magazine,* starting with the carriage ride that she and her soon-to-be husband took on the ride out:

> *We rode on like a prince and princess through fairy land, till we came to an inn with a sign of a black horse swinging in the wind. It was an old establishment, known to all the surrounding region as "Adam Howe's Tavern." The Howes, being industrious and economical, prospered well. Generation after generation of the family raised abundant crops, whereon they fed themselves and the public.*

Of the family, she says, "Gerusha [*sic*] and her father and brothers treated us more like welcome friends than like travelers stopping at a tavern. It reminded me of Dr. Johnson's remark that the best home that a man can have is a good inn."

Describing the inside, she states that she has very good recall:

> *The oaken floor was white with constant scouring, and looked refreshingly cleaner than paint can ever look. The looking glass was adorned with peacock feathers, and under it hung a plump pincushion in the shape of a heart, bearing the pins arranged in the words, "Remember me"...On the opposite wall hung the family coat of arms...*[t]*hrough an open window in the rear of the house came the fragrance of lilac bushes, and the pleasant prattling of a copious brook that ran sparking across the great meadow. Before the front window strutted a peacock.*

She provides a wonderful account of the dinner served:

> *The dinner was plain and old fashioned, like all else around us; but everything was delicious. The flavor of the butter was as delicate and sweet as the fragrance of new hay, and its hue was golden without the modern aid of coloring matter. The bread was such as can only be made by a skillful cook from grain which the sunshine has filled with saccharine.*

There is little else written about Adam except that he spent a significant amount of time researching the family history (nothing in the archives remains of his work), and he was somewhat active in town affairs. He served as selectmen and as a school committee representative in the early 1800s. Like his father, he also acquired property. Town records show that he received at least eight deeds from 1801 to 1831. Adam ran the tavern for nearly forty-six years. When he died on December 10, 1840, a great number of people from near and far came to his funeral, attesting to his many friendships that records do not reveal. Two years after he died, his wife and daughter would also pass away.

POSSIBLE CHANGES TO THE INN
DURING ADAM'S TIME

It was speculated that the east wing (Old Kitchen) was possibly a barn or another building on the site that was attached to the inn around the Adam Howe period. Since there is no documented history at all on this wing, no one knows for sure how and when it was built. In fact, the written evidence, though very limited, tells of another, more likely scenario (that it is much older). The first is an observation by the student Florence Whittemore in 1865. She writes, "The [old] kitchen with unpainted walls and bare rafters, brown with age, carries one back still further to the primitive buildings of the first settlers." If the east wing were relatively new (after the west wing ballroom was built), it likely would not show the age she describes (unless, of course, ancient paneling, flooring and fixtures were available to be reused).

A second observation is provided in a 1923 *Boston Globe* article written by Charles Lawrence. He states a belief from the Lemon period (1897–1923), "There are two small service ells, but in the day of old the great main kitchen, located in the east ell, was the heart and center of the house, and here, before the west ell with its dining room was added in 1800, mighty roasts and generous ale were served." A later landlord, Ford, notes that this east wing was added to the building prior to the west wing ballroom (in 1796). This comes either from the Lemon era belief or from Ford's own bevy of conservation experts probing the site.

A third observation comes from Harriette Merrifield Forbes, who writes in her 1889 book *The Hundredth Town, Glimpses of Life in Westborough*, "[The inn] grew gradually to its present size, the last addition being made seventy years ago [1819?], when there was a grand dedication ball."[43] It is not clear what was being dedicated; most likely, it was the ballroom (west) wing. It makes sense that a new ballroom would be a good reason for a dedication ball. If this was the last "addition," then it also implies that the Old Kitchen is much older. Horace Seymour, a later tenant, tells us that "this [west] wing was built between 1826 and 1830," so it somewhat supports the view that while Ezekiel may have built the west ell's shell, Adam perhaps finished it off in the 1820 time period. (Ezekiel's will states only that it is a chamber, not a ballroom.)[44]

Etching by Alfred F. Bellows (1829–1883) showing the inn likely in Adam's time (or Ezekiel's), as the large elm with the sign would be gone by the late 1860s or early 1870s. Bellows was from the Northeast, so he may have visited the inn; it is also possible that he may have seen an old picture mentioned in the 1899 *Journal*: "From a picture taken in 1855, we know that at the farthest corner stood a big elm tree. From this tree an old sign hung creaking with every breeze, and on it was painted the figure of a red horse." (The 1855 photo unfortunately is not in the archives.) This was the sign's first location. By 1864, it had moved across the street and hung on a pole by the barn. An 1867 Currier and Ives print hanging in the inn titled *Eventide-October* shows this sign location.

The Family of Adam Howe

Adam's surviving children—Jerusha, Adam Jr., Lyman and Abiel Winthrop[45]—are the last Howes of this esteemed lineage. Some old reminiscences give us a glimpse of these individuals.

Adeline Lunt tells us:

> *And the children of Mr. Howe were refined by nature, of gentle tone and manner, not commonly met with in ordinary country life. They had none of that coarseness of voice, or nasal twang, or roughness of diction, that characterized so many home-bred youths in New England. Their voices were of a quality that bespoke pure ancestry, and there is surely no more convincing argument for birth and blood than voice. These brothers were passionately fond of music, and…their gentle sister Jerusha, when she sat*

at the Clementi piano and warbled forth the air of "Brignal Banks" or
"Boonie Doon"…

Lunt continues:

They were, indeed, for those rougher days (as they were generally
considered), a pleasant picture of a superior New England family in
prosperous circumstances, of peaceful home-bred natures, exhibiting both
in parents and in children uncommon qualities of devotion, affection, and
good breeding.

JERUSHA HOWE (THE DAUGHTER)

Jerusha (1797–1842) holds a special spot in the history of the inn. Once
described as the "Belle of Sudbury," she is the only female Howe family
member with any recorded history. Her pianoforte in the Parlor became
memorialized in Longfellow's *Tale*s: "[The firelight]…On the old spinet's
ivory keys, / It played inaudible melodies."

Four fans in the archives labeled as Jerusha's. *From the 1995 Herbert Howe collection.*

Everyone who came in contact with her had the same impression: she was delicate, smart and proper. There are no known photographs of her in the archives, though one may have existed as late as 1958. Several of her possessions remain at the inn: the pianoforte, four petite fans and a textile picture titled "Labor and Wealth." This picture was reputedly "wrought by" Jerusha and given to a neighbor. It is not clear how the inn came to possess it. In the early 1990s, the artwork, along with the frame with Jerusha's name on it, was sent out for "conservation." It now hangs above the Pelig Wadsworth desk in the Parlor.

George W. Hunt, postmaster of South Sudbury in the late 1880s, told the story that "she had been engaged to marry an Englishman. He went home to conclude arrangements for the wedding but was never heard of afterwards. Miss Howe never married and died at the Inn."[46] This is the only place this story is ever mentioned; perhaps this is where the legend, true or false, began. George and Lyman were friends, so he did know the family.

An article in the August 19, 1872 *Boston Journal* remarks of Jerusha: "One thing however is certain, she not only persisted in living single herself, rejecting some excellent offers in her young days, but she also had a mortal dread that any of her brothers should marry and was a perpetual annoyance to 'young Adam' during his courtship with his first love…"

Lydia M. Childs, a visitor in 1828, describes Jerusha by saying, "Miss Howe seemed like one who had never been young and gay. Her manner was somewhat of Puritanical primness, and she looked as if she took life very seriously."

In Harriette Merrifield Forbes's 1889 article about the dedication ball, she further describes Jerusha's part in it:

> *Jerusha, "the belle of Sudbury,"—the only daughter of Adam Howe, then proprietor,—serving the wine and the pound-cake which she had made with her own hands…Should you chance to ask any gentleman who was a young man in Sudbury more than sixty years ago, if he knew Jerusha Howe, his eye would brighten as he answers, "Oh yes, I knew Jerusha. She was a handsome girl, tall and slim, and bright and smart." For a long time the little pale-blue satin slippers, with satin ribbon plaited around the edges, which she wore at this ball, were kept in the house. Longfellow speaks of her spinet—it was the first owned in Sudbury.*

Mrs. C. Van D. Chenoweth describes Jerusha in her May 1894 *New England Magazine* article, "The Landlord of the Wayside Inn":

Adam Howe, 1796–1840

Miss Jerusha Howe, the eldest sister of the Landlord, and years his senior, was ever cherished by the doughty Squire with peculiar tenderness, and her death, which occurred some twenty years before his own, remained a lasting sorrow. Fascinating stories are told of the fragile Miss Jerusha's beauty and her gentle manner. The old spinet of the inn parlor, the first musical instrument of its kind to appear in the town of Sudbury, was purchased for Miss Jerusha, who used to play upon it "The Battle of Prague" and "Copenhagen Waltz." She used to sing, too, in a thin and decorous voice, the sweet strains of "Highland Mary," so fashionable in that day. She had a chronicler's fondness for statistics, and maintained an unyielding hold upon the names and dates and events connected with her nearer lineage. The family record, as preserved by Miss Jerusha, held a place of undisputed authority among her kindred. [A few pages of this record came to the inn in the 1995 Howe Paper's donation.]

Adeline Lunt tells us in 1880:

Miss Jerusha was for that period far above the average country girl, and one might as well say of a later or present period. She possessed great common sense, combined with refined tastes, musical accomplishments, and rare domestic qualities. She had been educated at a fashionable boarding school in a distant city, and in many families of the merchants of the day she was always a welcome guest. She was delicate in person, and not much of robust constitution, which kept her much at home under the care of watchful parents. Her home was truly a happy one. With devoted parents, two brothers who worshipped her as if she were a creature almost too bright and too good for human nature's daily food, she was indeed the very queen of the mansion. While the other inmates presided over the domestic routine incident upon the bustling claims of a thriving public-house, she, like a sort of home Minerva, consecrated herself to the more elevated and graceful occupations, not neglecting those important functions among which was the weaving of linen for the household use…She pursued her quiet and maidenly duties without touching the roughness of life that was so commonly playing a part under the same roof.

The later years of Jerusha's diary are preserved at the Sudbury Library; the last entry was 1841. Jerusha died on February 2, 1842. In her will, she donated money to the library and a sizable sum—$1,000—"to be kept as a fund forever, the interest to be applied at the discretion of the selectmen

Jerusha's grave site near the front of the Wadsworth Cemetery in Sudbury. This is the final resting spot for Jerusha, her parents, her brothers and for Olive, Adam Jr.'s wife.

to supply the industrious poor in the town with fuel." The next year, the town found a way to claim this money and use it for other purposes, and the fund was never created. Jerusha also set out provisions for her elaborate marble tombstone, which brothers Adam and Lyman carried out for her (they had designed a tall, round column with a weeping rose inscribed on the base). She is buried in the Wadsworth Cemetery in Sudbury, along with her parents, brothers and Olive, Adam Jr.'s wife. Surprisingly, Rebecca and Winthrop, brother and sister to Jerusha and Lyman, who died very young, are buried with Ezekiel in the Revolutionary War cemetery (their name is spelled "Howe"; Ezekiel's is "How"). When Jerusha's tombstone was first put up, there was a rush to get the plots near it, as it was deemed quite magnificent at the time.

Adam Jr.

Adam Howe Jr. (1805–1857), Lyman's younger brother, built a house just east of the tavern sometime before 1830 (it appears on the 1830 Sudbury map). It was later called the Stoneleigh Farm, then later the Fallon House.

Adam Howe, 1796–1840

Adam Howe Jr.'s house a few hundred yards east of the inn. This photo was taken in 1900 just after the house was remodeled. Note the change in color of the roof showing the front porch expansion. The columns were not original to this house and were not there in Adam Howe Jr.'s days. *Courtesy of Heather and Richard Clement.*

He built this for his fiancée, who got ill and died before they had a chance to get married and move in. He was so swept up in grief, the story goes, that he fell under the spell of a maid at the inn, Olive Page. He married Olive in 1845 and moved to his new house. He had no children, but documented history is silent on the rest of his life. His property was bequeathed to Lyman when he died.

Adam Jr.'s house still stands, quite majestically, just off the eastern field. What one sees today is due to various renovations over the years. The columns in front are not original, nor is the attached barn. The house was remodeled in 1900 and "improved on" in 1915.

LYMAN HOWE, 1840–1861

The Fourth and Last Howe Landlord

Who in these days, when all things go by steam,
Recalls the stage-coach with its four-horse team.
Its sturdy driver, who remembers him?
Or the old landlord saturnine and grim.
—*In* History of New England, *by R.H. Howard and H. Crocker*

Squire Lyman Howe (1801–1861), next of the Howe Tavern keepers, is said to have presided from 1830 until 1861 (according to the old sign, innkeeper licenses cannot be found). When his father died in 1840 at age seventy-seven, the property was bequeathed equally to Lyman and his brother Adam. How Lyman ended up with the inn is unknown. It seems he was already running the business, and since his brother already had a house, it was likely the plan all along—or it just made sense between brothers. By 1850, Lyman would own 242 acres of land, while Adam would own 203.[47]

Lyman was Adam Sr.'s oldest son and took over the inn at a very tumultuous and dynamic time. Railroads were displacing the stagecoach and putting many taverns out of business (the Boston & Worcester Railroad sent out its first cars in the late 1830s). The Great Panic of 1837 hit, starting the longest and most devastating depression of the nineteenth century (lasting six years), and by the 1840s, Sudbury was becoming a dry town. The inn was still able to serve, but the overall climate for drinking changed. The inn and its barns were also getting older; they had aged another fifty to seventy-five years since his grandfather Ezekiel likely enlarged the structures to their present forms.

This was also the age of technical and literary discovery. Samuel F.B. Morse demonstrated the telegraph in May 1844, wiring "What has God Wrath" from Washington to Baltimore. The Hudson River School painters, the Transcendentalists and the other great writers of the era were emerging. Thoreau (*Walden*, 1854), Emerson (*Nature*, 1836), Whitman (*Leaves of Grass*, 1855), Hawthorne (*The Scarlett Letter*, 1850), Poe ("The Raven," 1845), Longfellow (*Evangeline*, 1847; *The Song of Hiawatha*, 1855) and many others were publishing some of their more notable works.

"Squire" Lyman Howe, 1801–1861. Undated photo.

Lyman never married, and as a result, the family dynamics so important in previous generations never developed. His sister, Jerusha, passed away in February 1842, and then his mother passed away in April 1842, likely breaking his heart. His brother moved down the road, presumably when he got married in 1845 or sooner, so the house was also getting emptier. Lunt tells us, "The Squire, now left alone to preside over the house, had not inherited any capacity for keeping a hotel, and the moderate ripple of business that came in those days to the house was almost too much for his facilities." There was a very old house mom, Aunt Margey, who presided over the running of the inn, although she may have passed away during this time as well. There was also hired help, including a Miss Eaton, who, a year after Lyman died, showed Longfellow around the inn. Lyman also had a faithful manservant, Buckley Parmenter, who was described as "the man of all work" and "nearing seventy." Buckley had a talent for biting a nail in two with his teeth. Lyman also had two dogs, old Pete and young Pete, that kept him company.

Nevertheless, Lyman ran the tavern for at least twenty years (possibly thirty, if the signboard was accurate). During these days, the inn still continued

Part of Lyman Howe's account book showing service, in 1856, to Professor Daniel Treadwell (who later became a character in Longfellow's book of verse).

as a business, combining innkeeping and farming. Lyman's ledger shows provisions of hay and space for as many as sixty-one head of cattle, as well as the sale of farm products including eggs, butter, milk and potatoes (his account books for the 1850s show that the farm brought in much more than the inn business). In Lyman's tavern account books, we also see the tabulation of room and board fees for a number of summer guests, including one Daniel Treadwell, who was later to become a character in Longfellow's *Tales*.

The historian Hudson tells us:

> *Squire Lyman Howe, the last landlord of the inn and the one of Mr. Longfellow's poem, was a man rather imposing in appearance, somewhat dignified and grave. He was at one time a prominent singer in the Congregational choir, a school committee man, and justice of the peace. Years ago, he was a familiar object to the villagers of South Sudbury, riding in his chaise with the top tipped back, as he went to the post-office or to visit the district schools; and he fitly represented, in his younger and more prosperous years, the family of Howe.*

Lunt gives us the most extensive account of this time:

> *Lyman and Adam were helpful in the farm work in a moderate degree, but not at all given to hard work of any description. During the winters*

Lyman sometimes taught school, and there was nothing he enjoyed more than to drill a class of boys in arithmetic. They were both simple-hearted and extremely good natured, and pleasant and genial in manner. Adam was unpretentious in tastes, and possessed no longings beyond his own home, which to him was the only place on earth. Lyman, on the other hand, had aspirations, and was fond of the acquaintanceship of superior men, and those of a higher caste than those with whom he was commonly thrown, as the ordinary frequenters of his father's house.

Lyman, universally called "The Squire," was somewhat looked up to in the town as a person of an uncommon capacity for subjects quite above the range of ordinary country minds or occupations. He served on the school committee, on the Board of Selectmen, and in matters of more abstruse character he was interested and well versed. Indeed, he was a curious mixture. He had natural brightness, but he was somewhat vain, and overrated himself. He assumed a pedantry with a class that might not know the meaning of the word, and yet discerned his boastful sense of superiority, which often made him their theme for ridicule. With one lofty science he was indeed strangely familiar—that of astronomy. On brilliant star-lit nights he was always with a telescope in hand gazing at the heights above, and not a star, or a planet, or a constellation, but he could tell you its name, its orbits, or its velocities.

There were other things of which he was vain; he was proud of his family, and of his coat of arms, which hung in the old parlor next to picture of Queen Mary, which was to him an emblem of future as well as of past honors, and he pleased himself with the thought of the way in which he might be received by the Lord Howe, of England, should he, the American cousin, take it into his head to cross the seas, or how some English maiden of high degree might be pleased to wed him and endow him with her fortune.

THE MARRIAGE BATTLES

Lyman's hopes of matrimonial bliss were also thwarted by other family influences. Jerusha's fears were one thing; there was also the problem of Aunt Margey. According to Lunt:

> *She was in constant fear that the Squire would be entrapped by some young and frivolous person, and it was agony to her to see him in such company.*

She was passionately fond of money; all the affection of her human nature seemed to have been brought to one focus in this passion. To guard her little stipend and the Squire's was her chief care, and she showed symptoms of liking strangers according to their pecuniary condition.

Lunt mentions that Lyman was "naturally of a peaceful and gentle disposition, abhorring jarring words, especially from women, he endured much from those who were his inferiors and his servants rather than have war." The spurned housekeepers were a particular problem for Lyman:

[They] *often proved refractory, and took advantage of his weak, pacific nature. Someone said that each one came with a determination to marry him, and finding this a failure; she avenged herself by torturing her difficult victim. Poor bachelor! He dreaded marriage lest he should be entrapped, but instead of being the victim of one, he was sacrificed to one every season. They treated him at times as if he were a little unruly boy. "Well, well, all women are warriors"—and seizing his telescope, his ever-constant solace, he would retire saying, "By Jupiter! I'll have a look at Mars!" and in this way he philosophically soothed his ruffed dignity.*

Lunt believes Lyman was not interested in the local country girls either:

The maidens, both young and old, of Sudbury town flattered the soft-mannered Squire. Indeed, he was deemed a bon parti; and yet had they but known, while he responded so graciously to their invitations, and joined them with his sonorous bass voice (another thing of which he was proud) in singing circles, the contempt which, matrimonially considered, he felt for a mere country girl! Squire Howe's wife should be city bred, musical to the finest degree, amiable, and accomplished. He had nevertheless, a chivalrous devotion to women, and the tenderest recollections of mother and sister.

Then she adds:

He evinced a taste for ladies of position—not rustic. And so, as years went on, the poor country maidens' chances grew less and less. For he continued a hopeless bachelor, and presided, en vieux garçon, over the old place, now sadly fallen from its former business-like character.

LIFE AT THE INN DURING LYMAN'S TIME

Lunt tells us about life at the inn:

> *A strange life it was, those days of the decline and fall of the old tavern. With summer came its guests—a quiet coterie that brought a certain life and air of indolent ease and leisure to the old place, which for the time was their own domain.*
>
> *The Squire and his servants occupied a portion somewhat removed, and the main body of the house was given up to the guests. The chambers were large and airy, and one of these that had formerly been a dancing hall, with lights hanging from the ceiling, a musicians' stand at one end, and seats placed for the dancers around the sides, served as a delightful bedroom for a July day or August night.*

She concludes with:

> *The very fact of the landlord being a bachelor placed life there on a very different basis from that which it would have undoubtedly assumed had he been head of a family, and everything in the regular comme-il-faut fashion. The irregularity of life, the contretemps, the bizarre situations, the humor of it, made it attractive from its very contrast to other households. There was of course a freedom of the house, and a management and direction of its affairs by the guests, that under different circumstances would not have existed.*

Lunt adds that most visitors did not see what was going on behind the scenes with the inn's "odd inmates" on the domestic side. She seems to have visited the inn sometime around the 1830s, when Adam Sr. was alive (or she just carries old stories forward), and she lived there for several summers with her brother, the poet T.W. Parsons, and with Lyman, so she knew it well. Parsons, like Treadwell, was part of the little group that summered at the inn and brought back news of these days to Longfellow.

A FEW MORE ANECDOTES ON LYMAN

The 1995 Howe Family papers provided the inn with information on an interesting buisiness venture. During the California Gold Rush of 1849, brothers Lyman and Adam formed a company with one Samuel S. Bacon to prospect for business opportunities (and gold) in California. The Bay State & California Trading & Mining Company was formed on March 14 of that year. Life insurance policies taken out on Mr. Bacon are also in the archives. Bacon sent a letter back to the Howes in September 1849, when he arrived. He wrote to the Howes about five hundred vessels in the harbor that "cannot git away" and that he was heading for the mines. How this endeavor turned out is not known.

William Parmenter, son of a maid at the inn, was born at the inn in 1854 and became a "chore boy." He wrote the following recollection of Lyman: "The Squire was a rather peculiar man, he drank quite heavily. He would walk around carrying a loaded cane and stamping it on the ground as he walked. He was afraid of being robbed and thought that this action would scare away robbers." (Most of the accounts of Lyman say he had a natural dignity, he was kind to everyone, and he was a public-spirited citizen. This drinking reference shows up only twice, here with Parmenter and below with Childs.)

Lyman was the real person Longfellow based his "landlord" character on in his *Tales of a Wayside Inn*. They likely never met. Stories of Lyman in the 1850s did make it back to Longfellow through a few of Longfellow's friends who summered at the inn. These friends later turned into some of the characters in his *Tales*. Lyman never felt the impact of the book, as it was published in 1863, two years after his death.

The End of the How Innkeeping Tradition

To describe the last days of the How(e) era, Lydia M. Child gives us some sense of the end:

> *I never saw the old place again* [referring to the 1828 visit]. *Years afterwards, Jerusha made me a visit. Her father was dead, and I knew she had troubles, though she tried to hide them. A shadow had long been coming over the sunshine of her home; the shadow that has enveloped so many homes in utter darkness. Travelers who stopped there to rest their teams were accustomed to call for strong drink, and the brother, on whom she depended to sustain the reputation of the old establishment, paid the penalty which so many tavern-keepers have,* [too much] *familiarity with the accursed thing. Everything about him degenerated from its ancient thriftiness, and began to wear a shabby and disconsolate aspect. Jerusha died, debts accumulated,*

and finally the primitive old homestead, with its fair acres of pastures and woodland, passed into the hands of strangers.

(Actually, it went into the hands of relatives who lived in Sudbury.)

On the morning of March 26, 1861, the squire was found "insensible" in his bed, and he died later that day (his bedroom was likely the room now called the Innkeeper's Room). Lyman passed away without a will and with $6,600.01 in debt outstanding. The house possessions and some property were sold to pay off these debts as the total estate was appraised at over $12,000. News accounts of the day speak of this auction and of how some of the rare Howe family heirlooms were lost for good (Jerusha's pianoforte and the old "somber" grandfather clock were two items sold off, as was the tavern sign).

Lyman died a bachelor, and with him, the long line of Howe landlords ended—John, Samuel, David, Ezekiel, Adam and Lyman (the last four at the inn). Interestingly, Cyrus Felton, in *Remarkable Events of Marlborough and Neighboring Towns* (1880), records that Lyman was the fifth Howe generation who kept the How Tavern. He somewhat suggests that this was based on a conversation the two had. What really happened in that early time period from Samuel to David (about 1700 to 1713) is part of the lost family history.

Wayside Inn in the 1860s. Seabury's 1914 *House Beautiful* article mentions that this is the oldest picture in existence of the inn, but likely it is one of four pictures in the archives from the same time period. This is how the inn looked at the end of the Lyman Howe era.

Thomas William Parsons, a friend of the Howes and Longfellow and the actual person on whom Longfellow based the character "the Poet" in his *Tales*, wrote a fitting poetic eulogy in 1870 called "The Old House in Sudbury."[48] It starts:

> *Thunder-clouds may roll above him,*
> *And the bolt may rend his oak:*
> *Lyman lieth where no longer*
> *He shall dread the lightning stroke.*

A copy of the poem has long hung inconspicuously on the east wall of the Innkeeper's Room. (See Lunt's comment in the Bar Room section to better understand the lighting reference in this verse.)

TENANT PERIOD, 1861–1897

From the Passing of the Last Howe Landlord through a Tenant Period

> *Never to his father's hostel*
> *Comes a kinsman or a guest;*
> *Midnight calls for no more candles:*
> *House and landlord both have rest.*
> *—T.W. Parsons*

PUFFER/NEWTON OWNERSHIP (1861–1893)

When Lyman passed away, the inn's ownership (and his brother's property that he inherited) went to his ninety-three-year-old aunt on his mother's side, Rebecca (Balcom) Puffer. She died four years later, in August 1865. Before she passed away, she deeded the property over to her two sons, Winthrop and Freeman. Freeman died in January 1865, so his half of the inn went to his children, James F. and Lucy A. Lucy sold her quarter share to James, and Winthrop gave James his share sometime before he died in 1882, making James the full owner. James is said to have run the inn from 1869 to 1883, though it is not clear if he ever lived there (tenants resided at the inn). Winthrop was noted in the *Puffer Genealogy* as having "run the farm" at the inn. When James passed away, the inn went to his wife, Adazalia (or Adeliza), who then ran it from 1883 to 1887. When Adazalia passed away in 1887, it passed back to Lucy A. (Puffer) Newton. Lucy was the last of this connected lineage to own the house (1887–93). Lucy and Adazalia may have lived in the house together toward the end of their lives. A letter dated January 29,

Picture of the inn in 1868. The Post Road is in the foreground. The old tavern sign was said to be hung on the elm at the far corner of the inn. Lightning strikes probably killed these elms, as Dutch elm disease did not come until 1928. This is probably close to what Longfellow saw when he visited in 1862.

1927, in the archives mentions a recollection of a sleighing party to the inn in 1886, which was then "owned and managed by two maiden sisters." For all these years, the inn appeared more like a deserted farmhouse than the renowned object of history and literature it would become.

Just before all these ownership movements occurred, Longfellow and his friend, publisher James Fields, visited the Howe Tavern on a beautiful Indian summer day in 1862. Longfellow had just started a new book of verse three weeks earlier and was probably looking for some inspiration. When they arrived, they were surprised to find it closed down. From this visit, Longfellow penned his impression for the opening Prelude of the *Tales*:

> *As ancient is this hostelry*
> *As any in the land may be,*
> *Built in the old Colonial day,*
> *When men lived in a grander way,*
> *With ampler hospitality;*

A kind of old Hobgoblin Hall,
Now somewhat fallen to decay,
With weather-stains upon the wall,
And stairways worn, and crazy doors,
And creaking and uneven floors,
And chimneys huge, and tiled and tall.

A few years later, on July 18, 1865, a newspaper of the time, the *Daily Evening Traveler*, described the inn somewhat similarly: "It seems to belong to another age: the very birds and flowers and bright sunlight around it seeming to make it still older and grayer, still more silent and deserted."

Eventually, when James took ownership in 1869, things started to turn for the better. He painted the house yellow, from its age-old, weathered gray color; put on new shingles; fixed the windows and doors; and laid a new Bar Room floor. He had plans to put up a new barn across the street, but he passed away on a hot Fourth of July day in 1883, the day before it was to be raised. The barn did go up, replacing the old large cow barn across from the inn.

How Tavern just after James Puffer's ownership (mid-1880s). Note the new barn to the right, what looks like a fresh coat of paint on the inn and the telephone poles.

Around this time (1884), telephone poles start appearing in inn photographs. A few years earlier, in 1876, Alexander Graham Bell had first demonstrated the telephone, transmitting "Mr. Watson, come here, I want to see you" from his lab in Boston to the room next door. The great Centennial Exhibition of 1876 in Philadelphia was held this same year, helping to reawaken Americans to their colonial past. It was also roughly the time that Samuel Adams Drake and the other writers started producing their nostalgic articles on the inn.

Tenants at the Inn

During the entire "tenant period" from 1861 to 1897 (including when the next owner took over), the inn no longer took in guests. It was a private residence rented out to three consecutive families.

Orin Dadmun was the first tenant from 1861 (or '62) to 1874. He was a local man and widower. When he got remarried, he moved out. There is little written about Orin. He was the tenant when the famous Howe family gathering occurred in 1871, and a large crowd of Howe descendants came to visit the inn.[49] Orin's nephew, Lafayette Dadmun, along with his wife and four boys—Archie, Hallie, Willie and Frank—moved in after him from 1874 to 1889.[50] It is not clear if the actual owners, James or Winthrop (or Adazalia and Lucy), ever lived here during this period. It has always been assumed they did not. From 1889 to 1897, the house was leased by Horace and Lizzie (Noyes) Seymour and their six children. Lizzie's father was a farmer on the property when Lyman was landlord, and Lyman used to take little Lizzie out on rides in his chaise. During the tenant period, only a few rooms were furnished; most of the house was entirely empty and full of cobwebs. There

Pictures said to be Lizzie and Horace Seymour (at different ages in their lives). The Seymours lived at the inn as tenants from 1889 to 1897.

was also a gate across the hall at the base of the front stairs, sealing off the house from dogs and hired men. The Bar Room was used as the kitchen and family room.

Right after the publication of Longfellow's book in 1863 (the Rebecca Puffer/Orin Dadmun period), visitors started showing up. All of the tenant families welcomed these guests, charging ten cents for a tour. (By 1899, the price for a tour went up to fifteen cents. Ford charged twenty-five cents in the 1920–40s, and by 1958, a tour would cost fifty cents. Guided tours ended in the 1970s; visitors are now free to wander the inn and grounds.) The tenants also rented the ballroom out for dances. There are several records of sleighing parties coming over to set up dances and being served oyster stew. Regular meals were not served, and overnight guest were still not accommodated.

THE LAFAYETTE DADMUN YEARS

Samuel Adams Drake gives us a sense of the inn during the Dadmun period. He writes in 1874 of his tour:

> *Conducted by the presiding genius of the place, Mrs. Dadmun, we passed from room to room and into the dance-hall, annexed to the ancient building. The dais at the end for the fiddlers, the wooden benches fixed to the walls, the floor smoothly polished by many joyous feet, and the modest effort at ornament, displayed the theatre where many a long winter's night had worn away into the morn ere the company dispersed to their heels, or the jangle of bells on the frosty air betokened the departure of the last of the country belles. The German was unknown; Polka, Redows, Lancers, were not; but contradances, cotillions, and minuets were measured by dainty feet, and the landlord's wooden lattice remained triced up the livelong night. O the amorous glances, the laughter, the bright eyes, and the bashful whispers that these walls have seen and listened to,—and the actors all dead and buried! The place is silent now, and there is no music, except you hear through the open windows the flute-like notes of the wood-thrush where he sits caroling a love-ditty to his mate.*

The most telling recollection of the Dadmun-era inn is provided by Lucie Welsh, who was the schoolteacher at the original Southwest School on Peakham Road in 1884 (the school was built in 1849 but burned down sometime after Lucie was there). Lucie boarded at the inn for roughly twelve weeks during the winter term. She tells us in an October 1952 *New Enterprise* (Norton, Massachusetts) newspaper article:

> *It was the Dadmuns who lived at the Inn in those days, and it was simply a private house, with perhaps a dancing party on Saturday nights, to which Mrs. Dadmun would serve an oyster stew. Mr. Dadmun was a teamster, and had several horses in the big barn opposite the house. My father went with him to see the horses, while Mother and I stayed with Mrs. Dadmun in the bar room, which was the living room for the family.*
>
> *Mrs. Dadmun was an excellent cook. Food was of the old fashioned, hearty type, and there was plenty of it…After dinner and a little conversation, Mrs. Dadmun led me through the cold halls to the room on the left near the rear door. In these days, there is a bed in this room, and it is wholly different.*

Mrs. Dadmun told Lucie, "This was Miss Jerusha's sitting room. She was the sister of the last Howe who ran this house as an inn. It is my parlor, and I thought you would like to sit here in the evening away from the boys and the rest of us."

Lucie went on:

> *It was kind of Mrs. Dadmun to make this room warm for me every evening. I liked to think of Miss Jerusha, who had sat here for so many years, helping her brother to manage the affairs of the Inn…she was company for me during the solitary evenings…The room was heated by a cylindrical shaped stove…when I was careless enough to lose the fire, I opened the door that led into the Old Dining Room but used at that time for a store room and wood shed* [this is the present-day Taproom]. *With trembling hands and chattering teeth, I entered this room and gathered kindling and shavings to renew my fire. If the moon shone into the room it was filled with eerie shadows.*

After walking back from school (about a mile east of the inn), Lucie noted some peculiar behavior by Mrs. Dadmun:

> *Mrs. Dadmun saw me coming and was at the door when I arrived. I heard the bolt toward the upper panel of the door as it slipped back, then the heavy key was turned in the lock, and finally the oak bar across the door was removed. The door opened to disclose my hostess, with "Tige,"*

the big Mastiff at her side. Larger than an ordinary calf, he was distinctly Mrs. Dadmun's dog, and was treated with respect by the rest of the family, including Mr. Dadmun himself…Right here let me say that this ritual of admitting me to the Inn was followed each night of my residence there. The doors at either end of the broad hall were kept bolted, locked, and barred at all times.

In those days the public road passed directly in front of the house, and the well and pump by the doorstone was used by teamsters, stragglers, tramps, and passers of all sorts. Mrs. Dadmun was alone all day and was naturally a timid soul. As soon as I reached home at night she told me in detail of all the people who had stopped at the pump through the day. In a short time she imbued me with her own fears. They were not wholly without foundation. I remember distinctly walking home from school one night with a group of three tramps behind me and two more at a short distance ahead of me. Worse yet were the occasional droves of cattle, being driven to Brighton to the slaughter houses. They would frighten me terribly, they would now. The bars, bolts and heavy keys are still on the doors of the Inn. They are evidently still in use. [The east wing entrance to the Old Kitchen still has one of these bars.]

The Dadmuns were kind and friendly people, doing everything they could to make me comfortable. It was no fault of theirs that the Inn as a whole was a cold storage plant, and the Lafayette Room, with its open fireplace, was a deep freeze compartment, in which the hot water brought up for me in the morning was promptly frozen and covered with ice when I went upstairs after breakfast to do my room.

THE SEYMOUR YEARS

Years later, an article appearing in the September 4, 1892 edition of the *New York Tribune* gives us an impression of what it was like to stop by the inn when the Seymours were tenants there:

The woman who greets you on your immediate entrance is by no means a typical English landlady or an ideal cicerone, she is plain Mrs. Seymour, the wife of a most estimable farmer, who "'lows that them poets and fellers havin' once bin in the house don't help to keep the wind out in the winter nor buy beef for the family." If Mr. Seymour was wiser in his methods, the fact that he lives in the Wayside Inn would help him materially "to buy beef for the family." But the

How Tavern, possibly 1878, in the L. Dadmun period. The dog might be their mastiff, Tige. The picture also seems to show James Puffer's improvements (yellow paint, new shingles).

ridiculously low price of 10 cents is charged to be "shown round," and Mrs. Seymour, who does the "showin' round," confines herself to gospel facts which in themselves are too few, and if it were not for talks with some of the old men in the adjacent town, one would go away rather sparsely informed as to the various traditions which center in this famous tavern.

Howe and Rogers Ownership (1893–1897)

During the last four years of this tenant period, while the Seymours were in residence, the inn was no longer owned by Lucy Newton. There was a rumor during her ownership that parties were trying to buy it and turn it into a "road house." Homer Rogers and S. Herbert Howe, local prominent business leaders, "did not like that idea so they decided to buy it" (this story was mentioned by Homer's cousin, Atherton, in his reminiscences). Lucy Newton sold the property to Howe on February 11, 1893. Howe then sold half to Rogers on May 16, 1893. Howe and Rogers owned the inn until January 23, 1897.

S. Herbert Howe (1835–1911) was a successful shoe manufacturer and also the first mayor of Marlborough (once it became a city, elected 1891). He was a descendant of the other (Abraham) Howe family in town (not of John). Homer Rogers (1840–1907) was a successful South Sudbury businessman and was reported to be an "ex-alderman of Boston." As soon as they purchased the inn from Lucy Newton, they began making necessary improvements of their own, such as performing structural repairs, painting, roofing and replacing some flooring. Since indoor plumbing was being introduced by the 1890s, it is possible they also had indoor facilities installed for the first time. (The first bathroom in the inn was thought to have been put into the closet to the left of the fireplace in the Old Kitchen.)

R.S. Newcomb, a later landlord's carpenter, tells us, "The lean-to at the rear of the old Inn was torn down in 1896. This was a small, crude affair in which they did some cooking." Atherton tells us that Howe and Rogers "changed the old driveway barn so the hill in front of the house might be seen," and apparently they also started accommodating tourists a little better: "Over the bar we served soft drinks, cigars, we also had things to sell with the cut of the house on them and also the book, the 'Tales of a Wayside Inn.'" House tours and renting of the ballroom for parties

S. Herbert Howe (top) and Homer Rogers, who bought the inn in 1893 to protect it from turning into a roadhouse. They started opening up the inn more for tourist but owned it for only four years before Lemon offered to buy it for $1,500 in late 1896.

also continued, but they still did not take in overnight guests or serve meals (though occasionally the tenants would feed visitors).

An 1895 picture of the Wayside Inn with some of Homer and Roger's restorations. The canvas awning started showing up in photos attributed to the early 1890s.

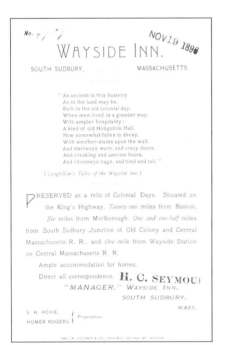

There is no information on how successful Rogers and Howe were on managing the inn. The Great Depression of 1873–97 was still having an impact on life during this period. Atherton does mention a plan to build a twenty-room building for "lodgers connected to the Inn by a covered walk," and he adds that "for a nine month period, they had nearly 5,000 people registered who were shown the house." For the dances, they charged a small fee and served refreshments, "and altogether, it was an enjoyable old place."

In "Sudbury, 1890–1989, 100 years in the Life of a Town" by town historian Curt Garfield, we read one small bit of information on this quiet period of ownership: "The *Lowell Weekly Journal* speculated that Ex-Mayor Howe's interest in the 90-acre property stemmed from his connection with a proposed new state central electric plan that would include an electric railroad from Waltham to Marlborough. Plans called for that railway to pass directly in front of the Inn."

THE END OF THE TENANT ERA

During this entire tenant period lasting thirty-six years, the inn's popularity seemed to ebb and flow. The centennial celebration came and went, and a handful of magazine articles picked up on the legend and lore of the inn. These likely helped increase traffic immediately after they were published, but the inn, it seems, never did have a grand period of rediscovery.

Lucie Welsh comments, "The people of this part of town were absorbed in their own pursuits and apparently had no time for neighborhood visiting. I have no remembrance of callers at the Inn." An observation provided in the 1892 *New York Tribune* also mentions "that no more people come to see the place is strange, for it is easily accessible from Boston or Worcester, to say nothing of nearer towns."

These accounts may not be entirely indicative of the traffic at the inn for this entire thirty-six-year time period; they are simply two of the very few known references to this era. When Atherton Rogers gives his recollection of the end of this period, his comments suggest that business is picking up.

Since the inn was not in total disrepair, it had a good location and at least some audience, and since the automobile was becoming more than a dream, there was hope it would survive and become a flourishing inn again. All the inn needed was the right person to see its full potential and one who could figure out how to run it as a sustainable business.

Before Howe and Rogers bought the inn, the noted author Edwin D. Mead wrote an article called "The Wayside Inn" for the widely read *New England Magazine* (in the November 1889 issue). It was a glowing review of the inn that included a plea for further preservation. It is possible that Howe and Rogers read this article and it factored into their decision in 1893. The next landlord certainly read it. Edward R. Lemon, a local wool merchant, antique collector and Longfellow enthusiast, needed a place to store his growing antique collection. Lemon was moved by this article and at some point started a dialogue with Mead.[51] In late 1896 or early 1897, Lemon made an offer to Howe and Rogers to buy the inn.

Since Longfellow's *Tales of a Wayside Inn* was published during this tenant period and his book was directly or indirectly the reason for the next landlord to step in, this would be a good place to learn more about Longfellow, his poem, the characters in the *Tales* and Longfellow's full connection to the inn.

LONGFELLOW AND HIS *TALES*,

1863

Famous now is the house in whose halls he hath been,
For his muse hath made sacred old Sudbury Inn!
—*T.W. Parsons*

The Red Horse Tavern of Longfellow's time is what inspired the famous book of verse. Using the liberties of a poet to mix fact and fiction, Longfellow created the romance and legendary lore of the *Tales*. The story of how this happened is a tale of its own.

Henry Wadsworth Longfellow (1807–1882) was one of the most beloved nineteenth-century poets in American history. A friend of Hawthorne and Emerson, his charm and intelligence seemed to endear him to everyone he met or who bought his books. Longfellow was already a published poet by the time he was thirteen. As a college professor at Bowdoin College in Maine, and later at Harvard, he published language arts textbooks (over his life, he became fluent in eight languages). His teaching profession also brought him to Europe on a number of occasions. After having gained some success publishing his 1835 travel biography, *Outre-Mer: A Pilgrimage Beyond the Seas*, *Hyperion* (1839) and *Voices of the Night* (1939), among others, he was wealthy enough to retire in 1854. Longfellow dreaded lecturing and decided he wanted to devote the rest of his life to writing. By 1858, he had already published several highly acclaimed volumes of poetry, including *Evangeline*, *The Song of Hiawatha* and *The Courtship of Miles Standish*. When his epic poem, *Tales of a Wayside Inn*, came out in 1863, it was no surprise that the first edition sold out in less than a month. His writing also involved a high level of technical ingenuity at which supporters marveled. He had his share of critics (including Edgar Allan Poe and Walt Whitman), but no one achieved more success and literary fame in their day then he did.

THE WAYSIDE INN AND LONGFELLOW

Twelve years before the end of the Lyman Howe era, a professor from Harvard (and friend of Longfellow's), Daniel Treadwell, was taking a carriage journey with his family to the interior of the state. When he reached the old Howe Tavern, he became so taken by the place that he decided to stay the night. He then decided he would summer there, which he did every year thereafter. He introduced the tavern to his Cambridge friends, among them Luigi Monti, Henry Wales and Thomas W. Parsons. They all came together with their families and made the inn their summer residence (though Wales died young, in 1856).

We know of Parsons's sister, Adeline Lunt, who visited the inn many times already and shared with us the vivid accounts of Adam Sr., Jerusha, Lyman and life at the tavern. Another sister of Parsons came to the inn and ended up marrying Monti. Upon this little group's return to Cambridge each year, they would have occasion to speak to Longfellow. When they did, the inn and their wonderful summers would always come up in conversation. Longfellow particularly admired his friend and fellow poet T.W. Parsons, and he saw that Parsons had already mentioned the

Henry Wadsworth Longfellow in 1863, when the *Tales* was published. This rare etching is by Alonzo Chappel.

Howe Tavern in unpublished verse. It is possible that Longfellow may have been inspired by this work.

Henry Wadsworth Longfellow may also have felt a special kinship to Sudbury, as his very great-uncle from his mother's side, Captain Samuel Wadsworth, was killed while bravely leading his troops against King Philip's warriors in the 1676 Sudbury Fight. Furthermore, Henry's grandfather, General Peleg Wadsworth, was a distinguished veteran of the Revolutionary War, and his uncle Henry Wadsworth (after whom he was named) was a navy lieutenant who died in the 1804 Battle of Tripoli. A sense of honor and pride surrounded the poet's family, which Longfellow may have seen surrounding the Hows of Sudbury.

By the early 1860s, Longfellow was already widely published and renowned around the world. He was so beloved in England that two years after he died, his bust was installed in the Poet's Corner of Westminster Abbey, the only American poet to be so honored. He had a style (use of catchy verse and colonial revival themes) aptly suited for this Romantic era in history (1850–1900), and his brilliance in writing allowed him to reach everyone. Edwin D. Mead, in the November 1889 *New England Magazine*, said of Longfellow, "None of our American poets has been more cosmopolitan in his tastes and culture than Longfellow. Yet none has been a warmer lover of America and American themes, and none perhaps has done so much to train the ivy over our history."

In the January 1861 edition of the *Atlantic Monthly*, Longfellow published his most famous verse of all time, "Paul Revere's Ride." (The poem was later to be incorporated in the *Tales* as chapter one, "The Landlord's Tale.") The issue appeared on newsstands a month earlier in Boston on December 20, the day South Carolina seceded from the Union. This poem was thought of as a call to arms, helping to rouse Northerners to action. It also helped sell his book.

WRITING OF THE *TALES*

Particularly noteworthy is that Longfellow's brilliance had to shine through some very difficult circumstances during the time his *Tales* was being written. His life, in fact, seemed to be as epic as his writing. In 1859, his best friend, congressman Charles Sumner, was beaten senseless by a congressman from South Carolina over the issues of slavery and secession. It took Sumner years to fully recover. In July 1861, Longfellow's beloved (second) wife of seventeen years, Fanny, accidently set fire to her dress while using hot wax to seal her daughter's curls in envelopes. Tragically, she died three days later.

Longfellow tried to put the flames out and, in doing so, burned himself so badly that his face was scarred for life. This is why he later took to wearing the patriarchal-looking beard. A few days later, his father-in-law died. Still later, in 1863, his oldest son ran away to fight in the Civil War and was shot through both shoulders.

Longfellow had produced nothing since his wife's death. The *Tales* would be the work to pull him through his grief. His journals and correspondence covering this period provide an interesting view of his emotions and how the poem developed. Journal entries in the weeks and months before the poem started are filled with lament for his wife and for the country going through the Civil War. When he reads of the Emancipation Proclamation on September 23, he becomes much more optimistic in his journal entries (abolition of slavery was an important issue in his life):

OCT. 11: *1862: Write a little upon the Wayside Inn,—a beginning, only.*

OCT. 31: *October ends with a delicious Indian-summer day. Drive with Fields to the old Howe Tavern in Sudbury,—alas, no longer an inn! A lovely valley; the winding road shaded by grand old oaks before the house. A rambling, tumble-down old building, two hundred years old; and till now in the family of the Howes, who have kept an inn for one hundred and seventy-five years. In the old time, it was a house of call for all travellers from Boston westward.*

"Howe Tavern" is what Longfellow actually wrote in his journal. His brother, Samuel, for some unknown reason, changed this to "Red-Horse Tavern" in his biography of Henry (he was known to have changed the wording of many entries). Most citations of this October 31 entry say "Red-Horse," as they use Samuel's biography as a source.[52]

Nov. 4: *Dear Madam* [Miss Eaton],—*I delivered safely into Professor Treadwell's hands the cane you gave me, and he seemed much gratified at your kind remembrance. Speaking of the old inn he said that on one of the parlor window panes were written some verses, with a date. Would you be so kind as to copy them for me, or any names and dates written on the windows? At Mr. How Brown's we saw the coat-of-arms and the old clock. P.S. Both Mr. Fields and myself feel much obliged to you for your kindness in showing us the old house.*

The letter to Miss Eaton on November 4.

Nov. 11: *The Sudbury Tales go on famously. I have now five complete, with a great part of the "Prelude."*

Nov. 18: *Finished the "Prelude" to the Wayside Inn.*

Nov. 29: *At work on a tale called "Torquemada," for the Sudbury Tales.*

Dec. 5: [Midnight] *Finished "Torquemada,"—a dismal story of fanaticism, but in its main points historic. See De Castro,* Protestantes Espanolas, *page 310.*

Dec. 13: *In the evening, Fields came out, and I read to him "Torquemada."*

1863—April 16: *Finish the translation of the* Inferno [Part 1 of the Divine Comedy]…*Meanwhile the Sudbury Tales are in press.*

(As soon as he was finished with the *Tales*, he went right to work on the monumental task of translating Dante, which he had taken up years before but laid aside.)

To James T. Fields*: Nahant, August 25, 1863…I am afraid we have made a mistake in calling the new volume, "The Sudbury Tales." Now that I see it announced I do not like the title. Sumner cries out against it and* *has persuaded me, as I think he will you, to come back to "The Wayside Inn." Pray think as we do.*

Nov. 25: *Published to-day by Ticknor and Fields,* Tales of a Wayside Inn; *fifteen thousand copies. The publishers dined with me; also Sumner and Greene.*

To Miss F. [a correspondent in England]: *December 28, 1863. The Wayside Inn has more foundation in fact than you may suppose. The town of Sudbury is about twenty miles from Cambridge. Some two hundred years ago, an English family, by the name of Howe, built there a country house, which has remained in the family down to the present time, the last of the race dying about two years ago. Losing their fortune, they became inn-keepers; and for a century the Red-Horse Inn has flourished, going down from father to son. The place is just as I have described it, though no longer an inn. All this will account for the landlord's coat-of-arms, and his being a justice of the peace, and his being known as "the Squire,"—things that must sound strange in English ears. All the characters are real. The musician is Ole Bull; the Spanish Jew, Israel Edrehi, whom I have seen as I have painted him, etc., etc.*

From Ralph Waldo Emerson: *Concord, February 24, 1864…What a fat and sleepy air is this, that I have never thanked you for the New Year's Poems,—chiefly, the "Birds," which is serene, happy and immortal as Chaucer, and speaks to all conditions!*

(This last reference is to "The Birds of Killingworth," one of the "Poet's Tales" in the greater *Tales*.)

LONGFELLOW'S JOURNEY TO THE INN

The only trip Longfellow ever took to the inn, as far as anyone knows, is the trip on October 31, 1862. Longfellow's biographer, his brother Samuel, had also long asserted this point. In fact, in his 1886 work on his brother, he specifically footnotes a 1826 trip Longfellow took to Albany that others have cited as a date when he also visited the inn:

> *It has been suggested that, as the Red Horse Tavern at Sudbury was the stopping-place of all stage-coaches going west from Boston, the author of the* Tales of a Wayside Inn *must at this time have made acquaintance with that ancient hostelry. He however made no note of it.*[53]

No journal entries in 1826, 1840 or any other date mention Sudbury or the Wayside Inn, and the 1840 date is from a misrepresentation in Alice Morse Earle's classic book *Stage Coach and Tavern Days*. In her text, she picks up on a conversation Samuel Adams Drake was having with Longfellow. She incorrectly turned this around into a journal entry, which it was not.[54] It would be from the 1862 trip alone that Longfellow would gather his memories and inspirations.

The Tales of a Wayside Inn

The frontispiece etching in the first edition of the *Tales*, Ticknor and Fields Publisher.

Longfellow's cast of characters included five people who actually spent time at the inn: a Sicilian political refugee (Luigi Monti, who briefly held a position teaching Italian at Harvard), a broad-minded theologian (Professor Treadwell, who was actually a physics professor at Harvard and not a theologian at all), a tenderhearted poet (T.W. Parsons, who was actually a dentist who wrote poetry on the side), a youthful student (Henry Wales, who graduated Harvard with a medical degree in 1841 and was a lover of rare books, which intrigued Longfellow) and the Yankee landlord (Lyman Howe). To this he added two others: a Spanish Jew (Isaac Edrehi, an acquaintance whose life was a story of wandering and hardship) and his dear friend the famous Norwegian musician Ole Bull. The characters in his *Tales* were all real, just fictionalized.

The adaptation of the musician is especially interesting since he was never at the inn, but he was prominently illustrated in the beginning of the *Tales*. John Van Schaick, in his book *The Characters in* Tales of a Wayside Inn, puts some color around this by citing a letter written to the *New York Times* on July 24, 1923, by J. William Fosdick, a friend of Monti's:

> *On cool autumnal nights, the inn family used to gather about the old fireplace, where they would roast apples and pop corn, tell stories, or listen to the fiddling of a farm hand who they invited in to make things lively. Upon his return to Cambridge, [Signor] Monti graphically described all these incidents to Longfellow, and the poet settled upon the idea of the convivial storytellers, the great fireplace, the fiddler, etc., and set about writing the famous creation of the Wayside Inn...The real musician of the Wayside Inn was the humble farm hand who used to help them roast their apples and pop their corn.*

The inn has in its possession two of Ole Bull's violins collected by either Lemon or Ford. They were restored after being rescued from the 1955 fire. They are not the violins "in Cremona's workshops made" (as Longfellow writes in the *Tales*, meaning a Stradivarius), but they are thought to be practice or touring violins.

As the characters sat around the Parlor fire over a three-day period, they took turns telling tales. Only the first tale ("Paul Revere's Ride") and the opening Prelude have anything to do with the inn or the area (the smaller Preludes to Parts II and III also touch upon the inn in a lesser way). In fact, only six of the twenty-two tales have American settings. The other tales wander off poetically on European-based themes. All speak of high aspirations, curious legends and noble deeds.

Of the use of this structure—using individual storytellers to tell their own tales—Longfellow "freely admitted," as Drake tells us in his 1894 book *Our Colonel Homes*,

> *that the idea of the* Tales of a Wayside Inn *was taken from Boccaccio's* Decameron. *The inn, he said, served as a framework for his tales. And he was equally unreserved with regard to certain deviations from the strict letter of historical narratives...he claimed the fullest freedom in adapting the story to the wants of his muse. This is nothing new. Thucydides long ago warned his readers against the blandishments of the poets.*

Unlike the *Decameron*, whose characters gather in a villa to try to lift one another's spirits up in a plague-stricken world, Longfellow has nothing dark underlying his plot; his characters are simply friends gathering from "far-off noisy towns" to "rest beneath its old oak-trees." Chaucer uses the same basic structure in his fourteenth-century *Canterbury Tales*. Instead of a villa, he uses a religious pilgrimage.

Writing of the Prelude

The Prelude of the *Tales* was the part that highlighted the Wayside Inn. Longfellow got some of his inspiration for this by a tour and introduction given by Abigail Eaton, a distant relative of Lyman's (through the Ezekiel How Jr. side of the family) and employee at the inn. She escorted Longfellow around, gave him her version of the family history and showed him the How family relics she had inherited. In his note thanking Eaton for the tour, we read that Longfellow also asked that she copy the writing on the windowpane that Treadwell had told him about. She dutifully copied the window etching of Molineaux and sent the notes to Longfellow. The Prelude, considered one of the classics of American literature, was completed just three weeks later.

Innkeeper Frank Koppeis in the Parlor pointing out the "fair Princess Mary" picture (a copy, as the original was destroyed) to the 1964 Dairy Princess. Adjacent to the picture are the framed Molineaux windowpanes. Behind Frank is the somber clock.

There were a number of relics bequeathed to Miss Eaton. These included the sword (or "Hanger" as Ezekiel called it), the coat of arms (the original, there were a number of copies made; the American Antiquarian Society owns one copy, created and bequeathed by Jerusha), a silk scarf of Jerusha's, silver spurs, jeweled cufflinks, shoe and knee buckles and Lieutenant How's watch. Also in this collection were a daguerreotype of Lyman and a picture of "Fair Princess Mary's pictured face," which hung in the Parlor (she was the daughter of George II). Over time, the inn has been bequeathed many of these items. The sword, watch, spurs, cufflinks and buckles are all on display at the inn.

Longfellow writes about these famous relics of the past that he saw that day:

> *The fire-light, shedding over all*
> *The splendor of its ruddy glow,*
> *Filled the whole parlor large and low;*
> *It gleamed on wainscot and on wall,*
> *It touched with more than wonted grace*
> *Fair Princess Mary's pictured face;*

And also:

> *And in the parlor, full in view,*
> *His coat-of-arms, well framed and glazed,*
> *Upon the wall in colors blazed;*
> *He beareth gules upon his shield,*
> *A chevron argent in the field,*
> *With three wolf's-heads, and for the crest*
> *A Wyvern part-per-pale addressed*
> *Upon a helmet barred; below*
> *The scroll reads, "By the name of Howe."*
> *And over this, no longer bright,*
> *Though glimmering with a latent light,*
> *Was hung the sword his grandsire bore*
> *In the rebellious days of yore,*
> *Down there at Concord in the fight.*

When Longfellow's book of verse was finally published in complete form on November 25, 1863, it was an instant success. A second series with extended works was published in 1870, and later a third series was published in 1872–73. Not surprisingly, with the title change from *Sudbury Tales* to *Tales of a Wayside Inn*, the old tavern was unwittingly rechristened and probably saved forever.

8

LEMON THE WOOL MERCHANT,

1897–1923

The Resurrection of the Wayside Inn

> *And tufts of wayside weeds and gorse*
> *Hung in the parlor of the inn*
> *Beneath the sign of the Red Horse.*
> *—Henry Wadsworth Longfellow*

Before Edward Rivers Lemon bought the Wayside Inn on January 23, 1897 (deed conveyed February 3, 1897), he was the Boston representative of the Sawyer Woolen Mills of Dover, New Hampshire, and Malden, Massachusetts. In his travels, he amassed a large collection of antiques and needed a home for them. He was pleased that his offer of $1,500 was accepted by Howe and Rogers, and Howe and Rogers were likely pleased that they made the acquaintance of someone who wanted to protect the inn as they had planned. Lemon was to carry on their work on an even grander scale, investing another $1,500 in renovations. More than anything else, Lemon returned the inn to a family-run business and restarted the tradition of innkeeping. Through him, it became a place of refuge and enjoyment again.

Charles A. Lawrence, a friend of Lemon's, wrote an article in the August 5, 1923 edition of the *Boston Globe Sunday Magazine* recalling fondly the early days: "Mr. Lemon…found the old mansion empty and desolate, with no furnishing except the ancient tavern desk and the bolt studded strong box that still sits beneath it in the Bar Room of the Inn." (The safe was brought here by Atherton Rogers; it is now stored in the archives.)

An 1899 photo showing E.R. Lemon (left) with Lucy Seaver, William Taylor and Benjamin Seaver. This William Taylor possibly went on to become the next landlord's (Ford) antique collector. Photos from the Ford era of Taylor bear a striking resemblance to this W. Talyor.

He continues:

> *But Mr. Lemon did much more—much more* [than just buy it]. *Being able to repeat from memory most of the "Tales of a Wayside Inn," he became acquainted with members of the Poet Longfellow's family, and in time gathered together a remarkable collection of things pertaining to the time when the inn was one of his vacation places. This included authentic portraits of the characters of the poem…and autographs, letters, and publications of them. Thus, Mr. Lemon had created an atmosphere of peculiar interest to all who love both the inn and the serene poet who made it famous…Finding there was no complete history of the place, he had also gathered a store of material for such a work, with illustrative material, and had planned for its early publication, when his passing, two years ago, forbade this for the time.*

Where this historic material ended up is unknown. It does not appear to have been preserved in the archives.

A 1928–29 picture of Lemon's sign and bracket. The current sign on the inn is based on Lemon's design.

Regarding the old signboard, Lawrence tells us, "Mr. Lemon found a very old [sign] board in the barn, but being so split, slivered, and battered by wind and sleet as to be out of the question for use." A few years later (1926), in a letter written to William Taylor, antique collector for the next landlord, Lawrence states: "Incidentally, I may add that I made for him [Lemon] a fair duplicate of his newer sign—the one which I presume is still hanging at the corner of the house, which he intended to have hung on the outer corner of the 'Gate House' which houses the old coaches. Together we tried to imitate the weathered paint." The sign hanging today derives from Lemon's classic vertical Red Horse sign. This sign was first hung on the inn in 1897.

Changes at the Inn

Lemon added many articles of antiquarian interest to the inn—paintings, silver and furniture—and while he retained most of the old features of the house, there were several notable changes made, especially on the exterior. He replaced the old decorative pediment and the canvas awning over the front door with an entrance porch (1897). Four dormer windows were added to the front roofline in 1897 (and at least two were added in the rear). Work began on four new attic rooms in 1898. These were called the Ole Bull Room in the northeast, the Treadwell Room in the southeast, the Edrihi/

Grain Room in the southwest and the Slave Room in the northwest (it is mentioned that "partitions" were put up in the attic prior to Lemon). Lemon also created the Parsons Bedroom out of the Old Hall on the second floor and the Washington Bedroom out of the How Sitting Room on the first floor.

In 1897, an extension of the service quarters was made off the back of the inn (now the first-floor kitchen), and then later, in 1916, it was expanded further with a brick kitchen (remember there was no main dining room rear wing in his time). The east wing was extended by joining the wood shed to it in 1904. By 1908, this would be finished off and become an art gallery with a balcony. A columned west wing front porch was added in 1906, and then a full wraparound porch and enclosed dining room were added by 1915. Lemon also built the English-style coach or gate house (finished in 1913). Legend has it that the timbers used came from the old Sun Tavern in either Watertown or Dock Square, Boston (both have been mentioned). Lemon used this coach house to house his collection of coaches and also as overflow space for his antique collection.

Lemon's coach house, completed in 1913, looking north. Through the opening you can see the edge of the garden. It was moved back across the street in 1939.

Lemon also installed the first "full" bathroom located in the "ballroom staircase hall" and added electricity in 1902. In the front of the inn, he replaced the old pump with a well house (1901). The house was painted a pinkish color with white trim, and sometime around 1908, it was painted a soft red color.

We can read a description of Lemon's inn in the 1902 book titled *Book of a Hundred Houses* by Charlotte Whitcomb:

> *Here is an omnium gatherum of heirlooms sufficient to stock a bazar. Braided rugs lie upon the floors, and upon them are placed quaint old chairs and tables. Here is an old-time safe, covered with iron half-balls, one of which is movable back and forth over the keyhole; and here are warming-pans, treasures of cups and plates in pewter, and utensils in copper and in brass; unique old lanterns, snuffers and tray, candlesticks, bellows finely carved, standishes, decanters, samplers, hornbooks, punchbowls, each article being of interest to the curious and of value to the antiquarian.*

The second-floor hall looking toward the front of the inn. The Parsons Bedroom (Old Hall) is to the right. Note the wallpaper and Victorian-era antiques. The Hadley chest to the left was destroyed in the fire. Lemon era, circa 1900.

The interior took on a late colonial/Victorian look. Wallpaper was added to almost every room, including the old Bar Room. This wallpaper was noted in news articles of the time as being beautiful and likely from England. The only room untouched was the Lafayette Room. Its noted "bluebell" wallpaper and floor stenciling remained from the days of the Howe ownership. Lemon's alternations and embellishments were a reinterpretation of the home and landscape and not truly a historic restoration.

At the bar, Lemon served ginger ale and tonic water (the town was dry; he did not have a liquor license). Lemon also started collecting some How family antiques, such as the coat of arms. He also collected the desk used by Daniel Webster while in college in Hanover, New Hampshire; two antique clocks; two chairs from the flagship Hartford that Admiral Farragut used in New Orleans; a chair used by John Adams; the washstand that Lafayette supposedly used during his stay; and two original prints by Paul Revere.[55] The Revere prints were stolen the morning after the 1955 fire. The whereabouts of the other antiques mentioned are unknown. It is quite possible that Cora's son, Edward, inherited some. Ford was said to have acquired $200,000 of Lemon's antiques.[56] This later landlord may have had many items shipped back to his massive antique arts storage facility in Dearborn. Some items, such as the Webster desk, were lost in the fire.

The Longfellow Memorial Garden was begun in 1905 as a tribute to Longfellow, as well as to inspire other artists. Mr. Lemon's sister, Ella, designed and planted everything with the aid of a gardener. It was formerly a vegetable garden. In 1918, Lemon added a bust of Longfellow that was a reproduction of the one in the Poet's Corner of Westminster Abbey (engraved into the right shoulder is "Erected by E.R. Lemon 1918"). The first thirty feet of the "west wall coping" of the garden were supposedly sourced from the old John Hancock House torn down in Boston, although you cannot tell by looking at it. (Another reminiscence mentions that all the brick came from that house.) The slate Longfellow plaque on the outside of the south wall was also put up sometime during the Lemon era.

In 1899, Lemon was responsible for having the main road moved away from the front door of the inn to a location twenty yards south (state planners were making road improvements, and Lemon convinced them to slightly reroute the road). This is now the paved Wayside Inn Road. The dirt driveway in front of the inn is the original Boston Post Road. A bypass of both of these roads would be put in twenty-nine years later.

To accommodate automobile traffic now starting to appear, a service garage was built in 1909. This was across the street, just west of the barn in

The 1909 garage located in the employee parking lot just to the right of the barn. Note the gasoline can in the hand of the rear gentlemen (possibly from "Standard Oil").

Electric Studebakers from 1904. Note the electric vehicle charging station just behind the first auto (it states on it, "Electric Hydrant"). No other details on these electric cars, or this day, exist.

The Wayside Inn showing the west wing porch. Lemon built the porch in 1906 and enclosed it in 1915. This wing would burn down entirely in 1955, and the porch would not be rebuilt. Note the old barn to the right. *From a set of photos taken after 1915 by Clifton Church for E.R. Lemon.*

what is now the employee parking lot. It was taken down in 1928. Records show that the first car, a steamer, appeared in October 1897. The electric Studebakers came in 1904, and the ubiquitous Ford Model T would start appearing around 1908.

LEMON, LONGFELLOW AND THE ARTISTIC ATTRACTION

As mentioned in the opening, Lemon was fascinated by Longfellow, and he sought to acquire all that he could on the poet and the *Tales'* seven characters. He must have contacted Luigi Monti, one of the real but fictionalized characters, because he received this (abbreviated) reply:[57]

Rome, July 4, 1898
Mr. Edward Lemon, Sudbury, Mass:

Dear Sir:
In answer to your letter of June the 5th I am delighted to learn that you have
purchased the dear old house and "carefully restored and put it back in its
old time condition." I sincerely hope that it may remain thus for a very long
time as a memento of the days and customs gone by.
  It is very sad for me to think that I am the only living member of that happy
company that used to spend their summer vacations there in the fifties.
Sincerely yours
Luigi Monti (The Young Sicilian)

Lemon's idea was to reopen the inn as a summer resort and mecca for
literary pilgrims. To do this, he started hosting a variety of literary and cultural
organizations. He especially welcomed artists, actors, students and literary-
minded visitors. The Fraters came (a group of Universalist ministers who
remarkably still come once a year), as did the fox hunting clubs and the Paint

E.R. Lemon in the Parlor, perhaps reading Longfellow. Note the coat of arms and the
Molineaux glass panes flanking it. Delft blue tiles are around the fireplace, and Longfellow
artifacts fill the room. *From the Collections of the Henry Ford. Used with permission.*

and Clay Club (a group of artists, poets and writers that included Alfred T. Ordway, Abbott Fuller Graves, Edward Filene and Quincy Kilby). In June 1897, just a few months after he bought the inn, Lemon hosted Samuel Bent and the Society of Colonial Wars. This is the setting for the famous oration Bent gave summarizing the inn and the Howe family.

Lemon was also becoming quite sophisticated on the dining side of the business. A menu from a May 20, 1899 Commercial Club meeting shows that the inn served: "Consommé au Jardinière, Soft Shell Crabs, Sauce Tartar, Fillet of Beef aux Champignons, Neapolitan Ices, Roquefort Cheese and Café Noir." Afternoon tea was also a ritual of the Lemon period and was served in the Old Bar Room. Lemon also became a gentlemen farmer, with a particular interest in Devon cattle. He owned the prize bull "King Philip of Sudbury."

In 1908, Lemon finished his private art gallery, made from attaching the woodshed to the east wing. His collection included a picture of Lemon's great-grandfather, William Lemon, painted by Gilbert Stuart. What happened to all his works of art is unknown. Like the furniture, Ford may have taken possession of these and possibly shipped them off site. The archives of the inn contain some artwork, but nothing substantial exists that is not currently displayed

Lemon's art gallery. Note the balcony above. This is now the Ford Room.

(there exists a short list of what was in Lemon's collection). Access to the gallery was through his private office, now the Innkeeper's Room. Lemon would take great joy in hearing that one of his guests was an art aficionado. He would lead these favored guests back to his gallery for a private viewing.

It was not easy managing the construction projects, restorations, budget and new visitors. Lemon was learning—just as past innkeepers had and future ones would—that the costs and time required to maintain this large structure were significant. Legal disputes also started for Lemon about a year after he opened. His contractor, Charles F. Jones, sued Lemon for underpayment. Lemon thought he was being overcharged. The case dragged on for years and eventually reached a settlement. For reasons not specifically known, Lemon tried to sell the inn through an ad appearing in the June 1902 *Country Life in America* magazine. The next month, he transferred the deed into his wife's name, possibly because some financial relief was found or a new legal protection strategy was devised.

A turnaround was coming. By 1904, some six thousand guests from all over the country had registered. The development of an affordable automobile and the jobs it produced helped bring greater prosperity to the country. Ordinary Americans were exploring the countryside more than they ever had before, becoming new paying customers. By 1915-16, the dining room had expanded and the brick kitchen was added.

A rare possibly 1917 photo showing the rear of the Wayside Inn before the Carding Millpond was created. This is a hay meadow, and during the How period, this was very valuable acreage. Now, the area is a pond surrounded by thick, overgrown vegetation.

An early 1897 picture (before the sign went up)—the good old times in the Lemon era.

END OF THE E.R. LEMON PERIOD

World War I shook the world from 1914 to 1918; its impact on the inn was not mentioned, but it surely was on everyone's mind. Edward R. Lemon passed away a year later, on December 19, 1919, having succumbed to pneumonia. The year 1919 was also when the big influenza epidemic hit the country. In 1920, Prohibition and the depression of 1920–21 started. Cora Lemon, Edward's wife, took over during this time and held the inn another four years, until 1923. It was known that there was no long-term plan for the inn, and Cora was said to have been facing financial and physical challenges.

9

THE HENRY FORD ERA,
1923—1945

The Building of the Site As We Know It Today

Lives of great men all remind us
We can make our lives sublime,
And, departing, leave behind us
Footprints on the sands of time;
—*Henry Wadsworth Longfellow, "Psalm of Life," seventh verse*

Henry Ford not only changed the world with his automobile, but he also changed the Wayside Inn. If not for Ford, the inn would not be in the protected and tranquil setting it is in today. While Lemon was wealthy, Ford was a billionaire, and it took his wealth to secure a fitting future for the inn. He is responsible for the preservation of the buildings and landscape, for collecting and preserving many How family heirlooms and other antiques used in the inn and, later, for turning the inn property into a nonprofit trust for the public. He also built or rebuilt just about every structure, including the gristmill, red schoolhouse, chapel, barn and even parts of the inn itself. It is hard to imagine what the inn would be without his influence from the years 1923 to 1945. After the 1955 fire, the Ford Foundation went even further by paying for all of the renovations.

Ford's aptitude and wealth made for a very interesting life. Though parts of it were highly controversial, he left a positive, indelible mark on the inn. How someone who brought mass production and technical innovation to the world could be so interested in the "old ways" is an interesting part of this story.

A BRIEF BIOGRAPHY OF HENRY FORD

Henry Ford was born near Dearborn, Michigan, on July 30, 1863, by the light of a kerosene lantern and died in that city on April 7, 1947, again by lantern light. The electrical system in his mansion had temporarily failed due to flooding on the nearby River Rouge.

Ford was a tinkerer and held several machinist positions when he was young. He spent his free time working on car ideas of his own design. He eventually went to work for the Detroit Illuminating Company, serving from 1890 to 1899, where he quickly rose to the rank of chief engineer. It was here that he met his mentor and lifelong friend Thomas Edison.

In 1896, Ford and a friend, Alex Dow, attended a company-sponsored convention in Manhattan Beach, New York. Edison was the guest of honor at the evening's banquet. Alex Dow pointed out Ford to Edison, telling him, "There's a young fellow who has made a gas car." Edison asked young Henry Ford a host of questions, and when the interview was over, Edison emphasized his satisfaction by banging his fist down on the table. "Young man," he said, "that's the thing! You have it! Your car is self-contained and carries its own power plant."

Years later, Ford reflected on that first meeting:

> *That bang on the table was worth worlds to me. No man up to then had given me any encouragement. I had hoped that I was headed right. Sometimes I knew that I was, sometimes I only wondered, but here, all at once and out of a clear sky, the greatest inventive genius in the world had given me complete approval. The man who knew most about electricity in the world had said that for the purpose, my gas motor was better than any electric motor could be.* [58]

Ford never forgot those words of encouragement. After that initial meeting, Ford was always very close to Edison. There is a story that says that when Edison died, Ford asked to have Edison's last breath captured in a test tube. Greenfield Village owns this relic, but the story and circumstances behind it are greatly disputed.

Ford's passion was automobiles, so he resigned from Detroit Illuminating. He started tinkering on cars again and sold his first car, the Quadricycle, in 1896. By 1903, he was successful enough to form what has become the Ford Motor Company. His firm did well, but in those early days, there were many competitors. Ford produced the models A, B, C, F, K, N, R and S, but his

Mina Edison, Harvey Firestone, Thomas Edison, Alice Longfellow and Henry and his wife, Clara Ford, in the Parlor of the Wayside Inn, 1924.

blockbuster came in 1908 with the Model T. This, he said, was a universal car ("You can have any color you want as long as it is black"), and mass production brought the price down from $950 to $290 by 1924. "Flivver" and "Tin Lizzie" were some of the more affectionate names bestowed on it. Besides mass production, he was also famous for the five-dollars-a-day wage—doubling the standard pay. This helped keep the unions out and made incomes grow to support a higher standard of living (so more people could buy cars). Later, he implemented the five-day workweek; he firmly believed that weekends were needed to absorb the results of this mass production. More than fifteen million Model Ts were built between 1908 and 1927. They were produced for a bit too long, as competitors did catch up. It took until 1928 for his next big release: the new Model A. With this model, he also significantly expanded production worldwide, including facilities in Britain, Germany and Russia.

Ford's obituary states that he retired as active head of the Ford Motor Company in 1918, at the age of fifty-five (as the richest man in the world). He

The Henry Ford Era, 1923–1945

The twenty-millionth Ford Model A in front of the inn, 1931.

turned over the presidency to his son, Edsel, and announced his intention of devoting himself thereafter to the development of his farm tractor and to the publication of his weekly journal, the *Dearborn Independent*. While never fully stepping out of the business (he retained final decision-making authority), he did begin pursuing some of his lifelong passions: dance, music, camping, utilitarian education, collecting Americana and promoting his views on the virtues of hard work and world peace. His cultural views were extremely controversial, but other books are better suited to analyze this part of his life. He also ran for a Senate position in 1918 to try to help his friend Woodrow Wilson bring about the League of Nations and peace (World War I was still on), but he was narrowly defeated.

There was a famous lawsuit brought by Ford against the *Chicago Tribune* in 1919 that likely plays into Ford's newfound desire to invest in Americana. It started with a number of articles Ford wrote in 1916 that were published in the *Tribune*. The paper then published an article claiming that Ford was an anarchist and pro-German in his views. Ford sued, and a public trial began. The oft-misquoted "History is more or less bunk" statement is drawn from this trial (in context, he was denouncing history from books, as he thought this recorded history was incomplete and, in many cases, misleading). During the trial, Ford was painted by the press as being completely lacking in knowledge on any part of

Henry Ford, Ella Lemon (Cora's sister-in-law), Cora Lemon and Clara Ford, possibly in 1923. The deed would pass to the Fords on August 9, 1923.

history. Ford won the trial (he was awarded a token six cents) but appears to have been humiliated and clearly misunderstood. He was determined to "show by example" what he meant by how to truly appreciate and learn from history.

In 1923, Ford bought the Wayside Inn (the deed was registered on August 9, 1923). A year later, he bought the somewhat similar circa 1836 Botsford Tavern, just outside Detroit. Henry and his wife, Clara, had danced at the Botsford in their youth. He started work on each as soon as he bought them. Ford visited the Wayside Inn a few times a year in the early years and then less in the later years, when his life became too full.[59]

And his life did get full. He started building Greenfield Village in 1929, a reproduction of the community where his wife, Clara, was born (now a major tourist attraction in Michigan). In the 1930s, he built a winter mansion in Georgia and established Richmond Hills as a philanthropic social experiment (a site that mirrors the Wayside Inn in many respects).[60] The list goes on regarding his other activities: the Huron Mountain Club, Ford Farms on the Fair Lane estate, the Berry School in Georgia, Camp

Ford in the Longfellow Garden built by E.R. Lemon. The bust was installed in 1918 and is a replica of Longfellow's bust in the Poet's Corner of Westminster Abbey. If you look where Ford is looking, you can see E.R. Lemon's name scratched into the shoulder.

Legion (a three-hundred-acre farming project in Dearborn), a summer home in Florida next door to his friend Thomas Edison, a new dance hall (Lovett Hall), forty-six trade schools across the country, yachts, railroads, shipping barges, coal mines and acquiring land in Florida and Brazil (in 1927) for rubber plantations (the Brazil site famously became "Fordlandia"). There are entire books written on Ford's other projects.

During this era, Ford's hands were also full with battling the new competition for his automobiles and tractors, negotiating labor disputes, launching an airplane division (1924–33 were the years the famous "Trimotor" was built), trying to help steer the country out of the Great Depression and away from World War II and pursuing questionable political activities. Quite interestingly, on August 28, 1939, Henry Ford was interviewed in the Edison Room of the Wayside Inn by a number of reporters. The talk surrounded the impending war. The next day, the *New York Herald*'s headline was: "Ford Says 'It's all a Big Bluff: They Don't Dare Have a War.'" In this interview, Ford went on to reiterate his oft-stated premise that a "back-to-the-land" movement was the solution to the world's problem (and that "at least Germany keeps its people at work"). He also claimed that his "new tractors will keep nations peaceful."

A year earlier in 1938, he had suffered a small stroke. When he realized that he was not well enough to take care of the day-to-day functioning of his company (although he should have been retired), he sold everything to his son Edsel, who, to everyone's sorrow, died five years later of stomach cancer. This brought Ford out of retirement, but he was nearing eighty. He retired again at the age of eighty-one in September 1945, handing over the business (through Clara's insistence) to his grandson, Henry Ford II. Ford died of a cerebral hemorrhage in 1947, when he was eighty-three, with Clara at his side.

The Acquisition of the Inn and the Plan

With Edward Lemon's death in 1919, his wife, Cora, took over the inn, but the responsibilities were getting to be too much for the aging Mrs. Lemon. L. Loring Brooks, a neighbor who lived in the Ezekiel How Jr. House[61] and a successful stockbroker, had a plan. He wanted to preserve the inn and its antiques and keep it operating as a nonprofit. He teamed with Charles Francis Adams, Massachusetts House Speaker B. Loring Young and distinguished lawyer and businessman E. Sohier Welch in forming a Wayside Inn Trust. Along with Charles W. Eliot, Allan Forbes, Henry Cabot Lodge, Dr. Myles Standish and others, they sent out an appeal to raise $200,000 through the sale of $100 shares. It was a good idea and gained public support, but it failed to raise the necessary funds. Brooks decided to take the proposal on the road and headed to see Henry Ford, thinking others would follow Ford's lead if he purchased a few shares. Ford was polite and listened carefully to Brooks's pitch but remained noncommittal. What motivated Brooks to visit Ford is unclear (Ford may have been sent a solicitation and responded in some way).[62]

Ford already knew about the inn, as his father was a devotee of Longfellow and had introduced the poet's work to Ford at an early age. Ford surely read about the old building, serene setting and the Howe family through the Prelude of the *Tales*. Ford had also visited the inn before. He states in several newspapers that his friend, the naturalist John Burroughs, first introduced the actual house to him (Burroughs died in 1921, so it must have been before then, possibly as early as 1914).

After the Brooks visit, Ford had his agents begin due diligence. That July (1923), Brooks was asked to attend a clandestine meeting in Boston with Ford. Publicity had to be avoided at all costs. They drove out to Sudbury to look at the property. Mrs. Lemon gave Mr. Ford and the others the full tour, and when asked if he'd like to invest, Ford said, "I'll take it all." A few days later, he gave Mrs. Lemon $60,000 for the inn and sixty acres of land. His agents were also successful in acquiring options on thirteen hundred acres of surrounding land, staying a step ahead of the anticipated land grab once Ford's involvement was announced.

Quite a number of newspaper articles in 1924 pick up on the story that Ford mentions one of the reasons he bought the inn was "because it's a small payment to Longfellow for four stanzas in his 'Psalm of Life'" (the first, second, sixth and ninth verses).[63] Ford mentions another reason for buying the inn in the July 1926 *Home and Garden Magazine*: "The Inn expresses the pioneer spirit—and the pioneer spirit is what America has, over and above any country." He adds:

> *I deeply admire the men who founded this country, and I think we ought to know more about them and how they lived and the force and courage they had. Of course we can read about them, but even if the account we are reading happens to be true, and often it is not, it cannot call up the full picture. The only way to see how our forefathers lived and to bring to mind what kind of people they were is to reconstruct, as nearly as possible, the exact conditions under which they lived.*

By 1945, Ford would come to own 2,822.58 acres surrounding the Wayside Inn (this number excludes other local Massachusetts holdings), making him one of the town's leading taxpayers. The Wayside Inn estate would extend to the tops of Nobscot Mountain and Doeskin Hill. In the *Home and Garden* article, he stated he created this buffer to keep out the "peanut and hotdog stands, side shows, and all sorts of catch-penny places"—but there was more to it.

THE GRAND PLAN

Ford's initial plan may have been to just buy the inn, but it quickly grew (particularly after meeting his soon-to-be principal antique agent, William Taylor). Reports started surfacing about greater plans. A 1925 Associated

The 1926 map of Ford's proposed development of the Wayside Inn site. *From the Collections of the Henry Ford, used with permission.*

Press news article reported, "Ford to Build Colonial Town…300 person village, living in the manner of our pilgrim fathers." An illustrated map of the plan has been preserved in Greenfield Village, dated January 1926.

The grand scale of the Wayside Inn property restoration was something that had never been attempted before. Rockefeller had yet to rebuild Williamsburg (1926), the DuPonts had yet to establish the Winterthur Museum (1951), Electra Havemeyer Webb had not yet put together the Shelburne Museum (Vermont, 1947), the Flints had yet to establish Historic Deerfield (Massachusetts, 1942), the Wells brothers had yet to open Old Sturbridge Village (Massachusetts, 1946) and Henry Hornblower II had yet to start Plymouth Plantation (Massachusetts, 1947), to name but a few similar sites. John D. Rockefeller Jr. actually came to the inn on May 6, 1930, to chat with Ford about the restoration of Williamsburg's Raleigh Tavern. As Ford's plans became even grander, the Wayside Inn became almost a testing ground for the larger-scale Greenfield Village that he was later to build.

Ford started accumulating a large number of local antique homes (roughly thirty) and their house lots and commenced construction work on other necessary buildings. He also started acquiring old mills, schools, barns, garages, furniture, tools, carriages, etc., from locations throughout the Northeast to be brought to the site (or taken away and stored in one of his eleven warehouses in Dearborn). While the full plan (if it even was a true plan), never materialized, Ford did establish a vast working farm on the property that included dairy, produce, food processing and food storage, with a goal to provide all the food that would be consumed at the inn. He created milling operations, a blacksmith and carpentry shop, a farm stand (store) and educational and social programs (schools, a church, outings, dances). Under Ford's stewardship, the property was once again an active working landscape as it had been during the How era. The fields and woodlots were being fully utilized. This was his utopian vision of the "good life." Pioneer values such as living "off the land," working hard and not being idle and good citizenship were the lessons he hoped the site would teach.

WORK STARTS ON THE WAYSIDE INN

Ford went to work immediately on the inn property and stayed very close to the activities through his personal secretary, Frank Campsall. He had William Taylor travel around the Northeast gathering the antiques

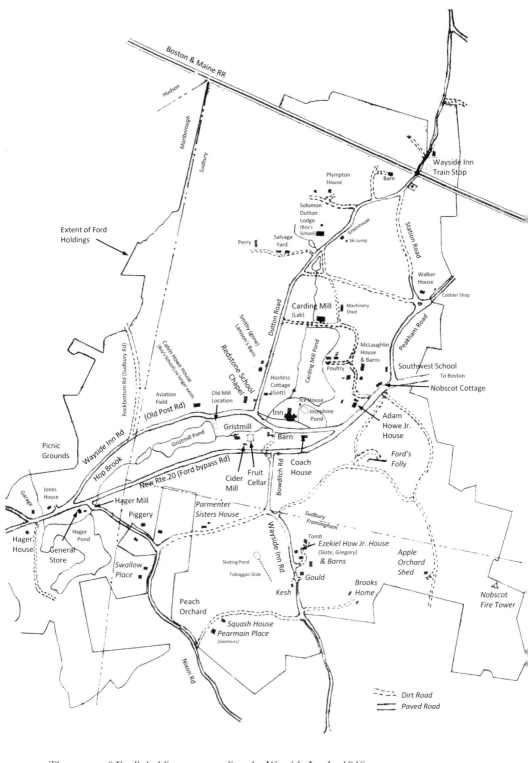

The extent of Ford's holdings surrounding the Wayside Inn by 1946.

mentioned (the Wayside Inn became the headquarters for collecting antiques for all other Ford properties). He appointed a manager, E.J. Boyer, to project manage the renovation work and to become the inn's manager. Ford also brought in preservation specialists to begin work on historic research to guide the renovation, and he had his people interview the three people who knew how the inn had looked before Lemon's alternations: Horace Seymour and his wife and former carpenter R.S. Newcomb. (The archives have these interviews. Many of the comments had to do with carpentry changes that were made inconsequential due to the 1955 fire.)

Ford's people unbricked the sixteen closed fireplaces, replaced all the floors that Lemon had not replaced, repaired the exterior, tore off the Victorian-era wallpaper and flooring, updated the plumbing, removed all the gas fixtures and turned the electric lights into historic, period correct fixtures and light bulbs. When a newspaper reporter asked if Ford consulted his friend Thomas Edison on the electric renovations, Ford replied, "You bet I did!" To honor Edison, he kept the best room in the inn as a bedroom for his friend (Ford named it the Edison Room; now it is called the Driver and Drover's Room). Ford brought furniture in that reminded Edison of his early childhood home in Ohio. (Interestingly, Thomas Edison's great-grandparents fled to Canada after the American Revolution because they had sided with the British.)

Ford acquired all the land and buildings originally owned by the Howes, including the three surrounding Howe properties: Adam Howe's house to the east (called the Fallon House when Ford bought it in 1939), Ezekiel How Jr.'s house to the south (1930) and the Calvin Howe House to the west (1923, then known as the Bright Mansion). He also brought back the Howe family antiques that Lemon had not been able acquire (the 1710 "somber" clock that he was particularly proud of, chests, furniture, the family Bible, signs, trunks and many other items). He restored the building and grounds and gave the whole area a new lease on life. As soon as the inn opened, Clara had the hostesses begin a "Hostess Diary" to record each day's activities. Clara loved reading these, and they continued on until her death in the 1950s. The entire collection is filed and indexed in the inn's archives.

Expansion of the Site

Gristmill

Being extremely interested in hydropower, one of Ford's first major building efforts was the construction of a new gristmill (1925–29). He hired John B. Campbell to design it and manage the construction. Hand-laying all the stones and the significant earthwork (using oxen to drag stones from Mount Nobscot and the surrounding area) caused the project to take almost five years to complete. The mill ground its first cornmeal on Thanksgiving Day 1929. Four quartzite millstones, weighing a ton apiece, were shipped to the mill from La Ferte sous Jouarre, France, and are still in use. The corn and wheat that is ground is used in the bakery at the inn and sold in the gift store and mill. The milling operation was one of the "industries" Ford established at the inn as a place for the Boys' School pupils to gain work experience and to support his "live off the land" experience.

The mill seen today replaced a mill near the same site that had been there since the early 1700s. The current mill is about ninety yards

The Wayside Inn gristmill in the 1940s without all the present-day overgrowth.

The Henry Ford Era, 1923–1945

The circa 1700s original mill site, looking south. The dam is just to the right. The new gristmill would be built behind and to the left of this mill. This photo is likely from the late 1800s, showing the shoe-nail and tack mill. Calvin Howe is said to be the man in the front.

Across the street from old the mill was the homestead of the David How Jr. family. This is one of the earliest known photos, from sometime in the mid-1800s. It was known as the Joseph Calvin Howe (1817–1905) House for a long time. The Bright family bought it before the Ford era and turned it into a small mansion. This photo looks west down the Post Road. The road in front leading left extends to the mill. Ford turned this building into a Boy's School. It burned down in the late 1940s.

downstream of the original mill site, which was right on the dam. The old mill built by David How was a gristmill by 1744. Its last use was as a "shoe-nail and tack" mill run by Joseph Calvin Howe (though the gristmill stones remained). The last mill was in rough shape and was taken down completely before Ford's new mill was erected.

Adeline Lunt recollects an earlier visit (circa 1830–50) to the inn: "The old mill (and is ever a country picture perfect without one?), ruinous and romantic, was yet near enough to the house to make it a favorite stroll for moon-lit evenings or sunset sittings."

She likely was referring to this old mill site, but she could have meant the old circa 1780 Knight's gristmill site a short walk up Dutton Road (where Ford was going to build a sawmill). In addition to the shoe and tack mill, Ford also bought the old Hager sawmill site near the General Store in 1923. Though he conducted hydraulic tests, the remains were in ruinous condition. There is no record of why he did not proceed.

What served as the design inspiration for the new gristmill is not recorded. There are a number of photos in the archives of old mills in Pennsylvania, so its design roots quite possibly came from that area. Campbell, hired by Ford to help design and build the mill, came from Philadelphia, so he may also have brought in some provincial ideas of his own. Campbell visited the mill again later in his life, when he was ninety-two. A reporter for the *Sudbury Town Crier* interviewed him during this 1979 visit. Campbell mentioned that when building this mill, "no expense was spared…the finest stonemasons [he could find] worked on the project," and "it was the finest job we ever did."

The original wheel was a Fitz Water Wheel Company overshoot wheel, designed to use the weight of the water to maximize the energy extracted out of small streams. This wheel was restored in 1972 using parts of the old wheel in a new wheel of Campbell's design. The wheel is eight by eighteen feet and geared up to 1:25 inside the mill (for every rotation of the waterwheel, the millstones rotate twenty-five times). The mill can grind twelve tons of corn in twenty-four hours, and the hydraulic energy output has been roughly calculated to be twenty-five horsepower at optimal design conditions. The millstones around the outside of the mill may have been collected by William Taylor, but their origins are unknown.

From 1952 to 1967, the mill was used by Pepperidge Farm for its whole wheat breads. The King Arthur Flour Company stepped in next and operated the mill at least through 1969, and possibly a little longer. In 2008, significant renovations were made to the wheel, machinery and roof of the gristmill thanks to several generous donors. The inn's miller, Richard Gnatowski, has been with the inn for thirty-four years and possesses a wealth of knowledge on this structure, milling operations, the Hows and the inn's history. He gives milling demonstrations almost daily.

Carding Mill

A second major hydraulic project took place on the same Hop Brook several hundred yards downstream (up Dutton Road). Ford dammed the Hop Brook behind the inn to create the thirty-two-acre Carding Mill Pond. At the dam he built a wool-carding mill in 1926 that was meant to be a mechanical laboratory for students. The stone basement was a stockroom filled with automobile parts and a Model T engine that was attached to a generator to produce the mill's power. Upstairs there was a carpentry shop, a forge and a welding station. The connection to wool carding presumably comes from parts or lumber taken from an actual carding mill in North Weare, New Hampshire, but there are few details

The carding mill on Dutton Road. Mr. Smith, the miller, and Mr. McLaughlin are shown measuring the depth of water on the weir. April 1930.

on this mill's history. The mill never had a wheel installed for reasons not recorded. A wheel was purchased later, but it never fit the site properly (it remains rusting near the mill). The Town of Sudbury now owns this property.

Bypass Road

In 1926, Ford's engineers determined that the Post Road outside the inn had too much heavy truck traffic on it and the vibrations would harm the inn (referring to Lemon's Post Road bypass built twenty-seven years ago; the original Post Road is the dirt driveway). Ford immediately started a project to build a commercial road that bypassed the inn entirely. When completed in 1928, it cost $288,000 (figures vary), and he sold it to the state for $1. This is the section of Route 20 that bypasses the inn. The Lemon paved road was renamed the Wayside Inn Road, and the old dirt Wayside Inn Road heading south from the inn was renamed Bowditch Road (it turns back into Wayside Inn Road as soon it crosses the nearby Framingham town line). Ford had a tunnel built under the new highway so he could move his livestock between the Wayside Inn fields and the farm on the Ezekiel How Jr. property.

Heavy equipment used in 1927 for the construction of the Route 20 bypass.

Redstone School

In 1926, Ford also began work on the Redstone Schoolhouse. This structure was found in Sterling, Massachusetts, where it was long ago recycled into a barn. The original teacher's chair and desk from the school were also found. Ford's crews disassembled the old school and used its timbers to build the new classic-looking red schoolhouse just west of the inn. It was Ford's desire to actually use this as a school for the children of Wayside Inn employees and other local children (grades one through four), so he successfully sought approval from the local school committee. It opened in January 1927 but closed the next day for a week because of a scarlet fever outbreak in town. The last class graduated in 1951. Ford was interested in the school because it was claimed to be the school attended by Mary Sawyer, of "Mary Had a Little Lamb" fame. A young pre-college student visiting the school was said to have penned the first few lines. The validity of the Sawyer story has long been challenged, particularly by Sarah Hale, a famed author of the time, who claimed she wrote it much earlier (she actually published it in 1830). Somewhat interestingly, "Mary Had a Little Lamb" were the first words Ford's friend Thomas Edison ever recorded into his 1877 phonograph invention.

The Redstone School building when it was being used as a barn in Sterling, Massachusetts. It was disassembled in 1926, and its parts were reused to build the red schoolhouse.

The Redstone School in 1930, three years after it opened. Note there is no chapel in the background. A small outhouse is to the left. Miss Allen is the teacher in the door.

Boys School

Ford then set his focus on an experimental school. He believed with hard work, strict morals and good instruction, any child could succeed. In 1928, he had his social workers screen the first twenty-eight boys to attend the Wayside Inn Boys School. These were underprivileged boys from sixteen to eighteen years old. The school was established in the brick Calvin Howe House just opposite the gristmill dam. It was called the Bright Mansion when purchased, but blueprints exist in the archives that label it as the "Edsel Ford House." It's possible that Edsel lived here, or had planned to live here, on his business trips to the east. The Solomon Dutton House up Dutton Road (now a private residence) was renovated to allow the expansion of the student body to fifty boys in 1931. Enrollment eventually increased to seventy-five. On December 17, 1943, fire destroyed the freshman and senior dorms at the Calvin Howe House, and Dutton House became the dormitory for the entire school. In 1944, the classroom section of the Calvin Howe House was destroyed by fire. The school closed shortly after Ford's death in 1947 and the

114

Younger schoolchildren dance in the 1800 Ballroom, likely in the 1930s or '40s. Ford established a program for all the children at his three schools on site to take old-time dance lessons.

Howe house was torn down. The Dutton Lodge was divided into three parts years later; the oldest northern section was moved across the street. All three parts have become beautiful private residences.

The boys at the school were involved in farming, mechanics, milling, ice harvesting, blacksmithing and carpentry. They were required to go to school half the day and work on the inn grounds the other half. They received salaries for their work and were expected to maintain savings accounts (thrift was an important lesson being taught). It was a tough school, but those who graduated always spoke warmly of their experiences.

As students, the boys had to attend daily chapel service and weekly dance classes. The dance instruction at the inn was led by Professor Albert "Hollywood" Haynes (a decedent of one of the original Sudbury settlers). Dances were the old-fashioned ones—waltzes, polkas, gavottes, quadrilles, mazurkas, schottisches and reels. It was Ford's belief that dancing taught the young men poise and "gentlemenness." Girls from the schools also attended this dance program. The dance held on Friday nights was the highlight of the students' week.

North Wing

To serve the crowds that were starting to come to the inn, Ford built a new dining room in 1927–28 off the rear of the inn (so as not to interfere with the inn's historic appearance), with a large dance hall above it. The 1955 fire started in this section of the inn, so the wing burned completely. The stone foundation was reused for the reconstruction.

The Stone Dam

From 1927 to 1930, laborers worked on a massive construction project, building a stone and concrete retention dam for the inn. The water, tested and found to be very pure, was to be used for drinking water and fire protection. Worth noting is that on the other side of Nobscot Mountain from this dam was a somewhat famous circa 1900 bottled water company called Nobscot Springs. It's likely that they were drawing from the same source, so it is no surprise that the water was

Ford's massive earthwork project to build a reservoir for drinking water and fire protection on the lower north slope of Mount Nobscot. This can be found in the woods off Bigelow Drive. It was filled only once.

of high quality. The dam still exists on the north side of Nobscot Mountain (southeast of the inn, off Bigelow Drive). Once built, problems developed. It was found to be built on sand, so it would fill in the springtime and drain by the fall. As late as 1946, they were still spending money to find a solution to the problem, but none came. The facility had to be abandoned, and thus it acquired the name "Ford's Folly."

General Store

In July 1929, Ford purchased the Parmenter-Garfield General Store in Sudbury Center.[64] His crews deconstructed this and moved it in two parts (using oxen) to a new site near Hager Pond on Route 20. It was operated from 1930 to 1938. As part of the opening celebration, Clara Ford waited on customers. The fruit and vegetable stand (now the east wing candy store) was a pet project of Clara's; she was the head of an agricultural organization that ran a country-wide project to teach farmers how to display and sell their own produce. Near the store is a small cobbler's shop that Ford also moved to the site.

The General Store in 1929 before it was opened. The building was split in two and dragged (with oxen) to this location near Hager's Pond. The second floor also had a springy dance floor.

The General Store, back when it was the Garfield-Parmenter Store in Sudbury Center (on left). The First Parish Church in the rear was the site of the first meetinghouse built on the west side of the river in 1723. The town hall is to the right of the church.

The story associated with the store's closing is interesting. Ford insisted on always having old-fashioned items sold at the store; no canned goods were ever allowed. On one visit in 1938, he saw a case of Campbell's tomato soup tucked away on a back shelf. He asked everyone to go outside, and then he locked the door for good and threw the key into Hager Pond behind the store. In 1947, Milt Swanson bought the store and ran it until 1971. His son Lee actually found this discarded key on the shore one day. Lee was later to become a longtime employee of the inn. The store continues to operate today.

Southwest School

Since the Redstone School only taught grades one through four, Ford sought and received approval to build a second public school—the Southwest District School—on Peakham Road in 1930. This school housed grades five through eight. There was a school on or near this site (where Lucie Welsh taught), opened in 1849, but it had burned down long ago. Ford had his antique agent William Taylor look around the Northeast for design ideas, and then Ford rebuilt the school to his liking. After the school closed in 1947, it was converted into a beautiful private home. The children from the Redstone and Southwest Schools, like those

The Southwest School, built in 1930 off Peakham Road. Housing grades five through eight, the boys entered on the left; girls would enter on the right. It is now a private home. A school stood on this site before 1849 but burned after 1884. Ford found a design he liked from somewhere in New England and had it replicated here.

at the Boys' School, were required to attend dance class on Fridays. The property just to the right of this house is still owned by the Wayside Inn.

Cider Mill

In 1930, Ford also built the cider mill near the gristmill to house the cider press. Large wooden screws and other parts were found in the structure, but there is no record of its actual use. In the 1950s–'70s it was used by the commercial mill operators to store grain. Today, it stores what is left of the Wayside Inn carriage and sled collection. A structural specialist looking at the original beams and other timbers in 1990 thought the structure may have originally come from Maine or the New Hampshire coast.

Hudson, in his *History of Sudbury*, tells us, "Cider-mills once stood in this district at the houses of Buckley Howe, David Howe at Nobscot [this is a relative], Micah Parmenter, Paul Walker, Capt. James Moore, John Brown, and at the Wayside Inn." These cider mills were established to produce *hard* cider, the commonest of all drinks in the early 1700s. Hudson also tells us: "The farmer wanted his extra cider for his hoeing or threshing and his extra rum for haying; and in the latter work he hardly

The 1930 cider mill with the gristmill in the background. Cider making in the old days was to make hard cider. The building currently houses the inn's collection of antique carriages.

thought it possible to get along without it. Many men and some women kept more or less in boozy week after week, and it is a question whether the larger percentage of stupid and stammering children born then, compared with those of the present time was not due to the excessive use of cider by parents."

Cold Storage Cellar

For produce processing and storage, Ford built a unique underground cold storage cellar (or plant) near the cider mill and gristmill. Construction started in 1928. Most of the produce harvested from the farms and orchards was stored here. It is a massive, one-quarter-acre, underground structure built of granite and reinforced concrete. Kneehole windows lined the east and west sides, and an elevator was on the south side. Near the west entrance was a canning room that also contained a cider press (the press still exists). Next to this room was the vinegar room. On the east side of the facility, there was a mushroom culturing area. The roof supports are all ventilation shafts; the boulders above on the outside cover the old openings. This structure was used throughout the 1930s and '40s, but it presumably was abandoned after the war once the schools shut down. Like the cider mill, it needs restoration.

Photo taken in 1932 inside the mammoth cold storage facility near the gristmill. It looks like a dark cave today, but back in the 1930s and '40s, this was a significant produce processing facility. This picture shows the cider press in the canning room (located near the west entrance).

Apple Orchard

Ford's property included a 237-acre apple orchard (he had sixteen hundred trees planted) across from the inn up the side of Nobscot Mountain. It sustained the inn with produce for many years, but through the war years, it was neglected. By 1946, it was said that two-thirds of the property was overgrown with brush, and the treetops had not been pruned in years. In recent years, a housing development was planned on the site, but the discovery of large amounts of arsenic from the pesticides in the soil apparently made the site unbuildable. Ford's orchard was built on, or close to, the old Indian orchards dating back to the 1600s (then owned by Tantamous and Peter Jethro).

Icehouse

When Ford bought the property, he had the icehouse pond excavated and built a new icehouse next to the older, smaller one. He named the pond Josephine Pond, after one of his granddaughters who is said to have fallen into it. Ice harvesting led by the miller, Richard Gnatowski, along with his Friends of Grist (FOG) organization, is demonstrated in February.

Boys' School students harvesting ice on Josephine Pond, early 1930s.

Lemon's coach house in its original location across from the garden before Ford had it moved in 1939. A barn once stood on or near this site.

Coach/Gate House

To gain a better view of the estate, Ford moved the Lemon coach house in 1939 from near the garden to its present location across Wayside Inn Road. It continued to house the coaches. It was the innkeeper's office for several years, and then by 1951, it was turned into an antique store, selling off excess antiques from Greenfield Village. By the 1960s, the center stall was closed off, and it garaged the Wayside Inn fire truck. Presently, the building is used as an apartment for one of the inn's employees and for storage.

Chapel

The great hurricane of 1938 toppled a stand of tall white pine trees on the hill behind the Redstone School. These trees provided the wood to construct the next part of Ford's plan: the Martha-Mary Chapel (named after both Clara and Henry's mothers, Martha Bryant and Mary Ford). Construction started in 1939 with the laying of a massive stone foundation. Boys and girls from the schools were involved in the construction. The chandelier is reportedly eighteenth-century English, installed in 1946. The steeple is a replica of the one on the First Church of Christ in Bradford, Massachusetts. One of Ford's antique agents discovered this in 1927, and Ford himself went to take a look. He liked it so much that he used this design on his first chapel in Greenfield Village (1929) and on three more of the six Martha-Mary Chapels he built (Sudbury's was his fifth chapel but widely acclaimed to be his finest). The wrought-iron weather vane was placed on the steeple on July 30, 1940, Ford's seventy-seventh birthday. It came down in a storm in the early 2000s. It was

Hoisting the steeple up on the chapel, 1939. The chapel would be finished in 1940. This would be Ford's fifth of the six Martha-Mary Chapels he built.

replaced with a new one during the 2006–8 construction that turned the chapel steeple into one very large cellphone tower for three carriers. Telecom equipment cabinets now fill a good part of the basement. Roughly 110 weddings a year are booked for this picturesque chapel, which seats 150 people. Besides weddings, it is also used as a concert hall. When built, the chapel was meant to be used by pupils of the Ford schools on the property. They had a daily attendance requirement for morning service, and the basement was used for dances.

Other Structures

Ford bought and renovated a number of other structures, including the three How houses already mentioned, the Old Walker House, the Jones House/Tavern, the Hager House and the Nobscot Teahouse and Tavern (the gambrel tavern part was moved by Ford from the Hager House just down the street in Marlborough). He also bought and renovated the

The Ezekiel How Jr. House, front view, mid-1800s. This was a smaller version of the Wayside Inn, up Bowditch/Wayside Inn Road, not far away, and is now fully restored as a private home. Ezekiel Jr. was a Patriot, participating in battles at Concord, White Plains and Saratoga. *Photo Courtesy of Tony Howes.*

Sparrow House, the Parmenter Sisters' House and the Hostess Cottage (used for the female inn hostesses). All of these old houses are now private residences. One house, the circa 1700 Plympton House on Dutton Road, was disassembled and moved to Greenfield Village. In addition to old buildings and antiques, Ford also started collecting farm tools, sleds, carriages and farm stock.

Four major barn complexes existed at this site: the dairy barn at Ezekiel How Jr.'s house, the Parmenter/McLaughlin Farm behind the Adam Howe House (labeled as "young stock barns" on some maps), the Calvin Howe property farm (which burned down before 1931) and Lamson's Farm on Dutton Road. Ford's overall herd once consisted of approximately 31 head of Devon cattle, at least 6 oxen, 76 Cheviot sheep (pastured across from the inn and by the gristmill) and 42 goats (pastured on Dutton Road). The inn's poultry range near the dairy barn housed a flock of 1,259 white leghorn chickens and 77 turkey poults. The piggery on Hager Road near the apple and peach orchards housed 24 Berkshire hogs.

Other Plans

There were plans in the works for two other structures. In 1941, a large sawmill was to be built on the stream across from Dutton Lodge, on or near the site of the old gristmill shown on the 1794 Sudbury map. A blacksmith shop was to be placed somewhere. Ford purchased an ancient, dilapidated blacksmith shop in Georgetown, Massachusetts, to be moved to Sudbury, but what became of it is unknown. The only blacksmith shop built was in the salvage yard near the Boys' School on Dutton Road, a twenty-four- by eighteen-foot structure. There is a "smithy" marked on the Ford-era map on Dutton Road, but there is no record, nor any collective knowledge, about that being a blacksmith shop.

To provide the wood for all his restoration work, Ford had a large sawmill constructed in the field across from the inn behind the gristmill. This was erected in 1925 and moved when the mill was completed. It was then set up behind the General Store to process all the logs floating in Hager Pond after the hurricane.

Ford did have a plan in 1926 to buy the Charles O. Parmenter Gristmill (in the Mill Village section of Sudbury) and the water rights to create a "village industries" complex (known as the Wash Brook Project). Here, reportedly, Ford wanted to build a large plant to manufacture Bakelite dashboard parts. The intent and facts of this are disputed; he certainly would need more power than what the mill could provide. Ford started buying options on the land, but one holdout with a key piece of real estate stopped the deal. The existing mill on the site burned down in 1927, complicating the efforts, and Ford finally just pulled out. Ford also bought two hundred acres of land near Mirror Lake on the Sudbury-Stow line for a possible airport and airplane parts factory in 1928. This was never developed, and the land was given to the government.

FORD COACHES AND CARRIAGES

Ford's vision for the site was to use as much "pioneering" labor as possible. This included the use of oxen and horses whenever possible. The archives are filled with photographs of the animals and the carts. There were tipcarts, manure carts, wood and other carts, large winter sleighs, buggies, carriages, and one-horse shays. Some came from Lemon, but most came through Ford acquisitions. Many still exist in the Wayside Inn collection and are stored on site, and most need serious restoration work. Ford had three horse coaches: the Lafayette coach inherited from Lemon (which was sold in 1995 for one dollar to the Shirley-Eustis House), an Abbott

A circa 1850 Abbott and Dowling Concord coach acquired by Ford. This one was actually used for the Worcester-to-Marlboro circuit in the day of the stage. It was "restored" in 1974 and is still owned by the inn. There is a record of Ford acquiring at least three Concord coaches, but only one has ever been seen.

and Downing Concord coach that actually served the Marlborough-Worcester stage circuit (it was restored in 1974 and ceremoniously ridden back by horse from New Hampshire, where the work was done) and a third coach that shows up in a few pictures but whose history is unclear. It could have been the circa 1831 Sibly "Bear Camp River Coach." There are many pictures of the coaches and carriages used by Ford, but few records documenting them exist.

OTHER FORD ACTIVITY AT THE INN

On one early visit to the inn before he bought it, or possibly just after, Ford met members of the Millwood Hunt Club, a foxhunting club resurrected by the Bowditch family from just over the hill in Framingham. He took a strong liking to members of this group, even inviting them to his exclusive opening party in February 1924. Later, he gave the group full access to the property and had his workmen help clear horse paths. The Norfolk Hunt of Dover and the Middlesex Hunt of South Lincoln were also hunt clubs that began using the property.

The Millwood Hunt Club getting ready for a fox and hound hunt, 1924.

Space does not permit a telling of all the interesting events held at the inn. The Hostess Diaries, a voluminous record of daily activity at the inn, records everything—from 4H farmers' picnics to all the distinguished guests. In Ford's time, they charged twenty-five cents to tour the house, and no liquor or tipping was allowed. Ford also had a rule that no priest, minister, nun or religious leader would ever pay for dinner at the inn.

Ford's love of dance is what led him to be introduced to Benjamin Lovett of Hudson, Massachusetts. Lovett was the Wayside Inn's semi-contracted dance instructor. After they met in 1923, Ford hired Mr. Lovett, not just to call and organize dances (primarily back in Michigan, where Lovett had to move), but also to help integrate dance into his schools and whatever other public schools would listen (and take his money). He deeply admired Mr. Lovett and named a new dance hall in Greenfield Village after him. Ford and Lovett published at least two dance books together. One recorded fanciful story says that he tried to hire Lovett away from the inn before he bought the place. Lovett felt he needed to honor his contract with the inn and said no, so Ford, it was said, bought the inn to get Lovett.[65]

The End of the Era

Indeed, Ford's hands were full, as were the hands of his family members who were busy trying to keep the Ford Company prosperous after years of mismanagement and alleged criminal conduct. Times were also changing; the war ended, and people wanted to move forward into modern times. It was decided that Henry and Clara would place the historic Wayside Inn into a protective nonprofit trust. There was no endowment; the inn would have to create a business model that was self-sustaining. Ford family members were the first board members of the trust, so it did have a small helping hand to start.

10

THE MODERN ERA, 1945–TODAY

Trust through Koppeis to the Present

Along the varying road of life,
In calm content, in toil or strife,
In morn or at noon, by night or day,
How oft doth man by care oppressed
Find at an inn a place of rest!
—William Combe

Ford understandably could not keep his focus on the inn late in his life, and Clara was in love with her Dearborn home, Fair Lane, and the Richmond Hill estate (Clara would pass away three years after Henry). The war changed everyone's priorities, and the Ford Motor Company needed to be righted after several years of neglect. In a generous move that reflects Ford's earlier announced intention, Henry and Clara Ford decided to place the inn in a charitable trust so it could be forever preserved. On November 2, 1944, they created the Wayside Inn Trust and donated to it the inn proper and its immediate surrounding land, and the next year, on November 13, 1945, they deeded over the rest of the property.

Despite the enthusiasm to continue on with the preservation mission of the inn, the post-war years were not very profitable. In 1946, an appraisal was done to assess what parts of the Wayside Inn estate could be sold to help pay the bills. This report in the archives mentions that on the entire estate (except the inn), "only the Jones, Walker, and Parmenter Place are livable." Most of the other structures were listed as being in fair condition (by 1946 standards). Approximately 2,300 acres were sold off between 1946 and 1951, most with restrictions, and then, little by little, the trustees sold off other properties. The inn property today is approximately 125 acres, roughly the same area that was transferred to the trust in 1944.

The inn closed for the winter months of December 1950 to April 1951 because there was not enough business to sustain its operation. The inn manager was even forced to advise waitresses and kitchen staff to start making smaller portions and charging for additional coffee and desserts. Free dinners for religious leaders and tour bus drivers also ended. By 1953, a liquor license had been procured, the first since the days of Lyman Howe, but this was costly, and the inn entered the 1953 summer season in debt.

Then came the disastrous fire of December 21, 1955. It started in the boiler of the north wing and brought down three quarters of the inn. No fire hydrants were in the area of the inn, so a hole had to be painstakingly chipped through the thick ice of Josephine Pond to extract water. By morning, it was drained completely. The north and west wings were completely lost. The main building suffered significant damage. The east wing with the Old Kitchen pulled through with only smoke damage. Many of the antiques were lost, but fortunately, the frigid temperature outside turned the water used to extinguish the fire into a protective coat of ice over some furniture and artifacts, helping preserve them (such as the circa 1675 center table in the Bar Room, the coat of arms and the Molineaux glass).

The fire was widely publicized, and the outcry to rebuild started right away. Donations quickly poured in. The Ford family, through the trust, stepped in and donated the full $675,000 needed to restore the inn property. The trust then set about to return whatever donations it could. To restore the inn properly, it hired Dr. Donald Shelly from Greenfield Village and Ralph

Fire engulfing the ballroom, December 21, 1955. By morning, three quarters of the inn would be heavily damaged. The fire would start in the boiler room in the north wing.

The Modern Era, 1945–Today

The Old Dining Room and the Lafayette Bedroom above were gutted during the fire. The Old Kitchen is through the door to the left. Fortunately, it suffered only smoke damage.

Looking into space that would become the reconstructed bar (southeast corner). The front door is to right of photo.

Carpenter, a noted New England restoration specialist, to study the inn and create a plan for its full restoration. Preserving as much of the old structure as possible was one of the primary objectives. With such a long history, the first challenge was to figure out what period should they restore it back to—the colonial era, the late colonial/Longfellow time or the more recent Lemon/

Ford period? The late colonial period, close to what Longfellow may have seen, was felt to be the period that would serve the site best. The Lemon era dormers and porches would not be replaced, nor would the attic rooms and Ford's large hall. Carpenter and the trustees then hired Roy Baker of Antrim, New Hampshire, an expert post-and-beam carpenter well known to the Society for the Preservation of New England Antiquities (SPNEA), to lead the reconstruction.

After the fire, the trust was also determined to improve the business of the inn by integrating better kitchen, dining and guest facilities. This was done with a new design for the north wing. When rebuilt on the same foundation, it now contained eight new guest rooms on the second floor, a dining room on the first floor and a new kitchen in the basement. On June 7, 1958, the inn was reopened following two and a half years of research and

The freshly minted inn in 1958, soon after the reconstruction was completed. Note the gift shop sign hanging in front of the east wing (Old Kitchen) door. Out of the picture farther to the right hung another sign advertising the Red Horse Cocktail Room (these came down in the early 1960s). The entrance walkway would change in 2011 when a new brick walk was added to replace the wood planks (and these bushes) that had been on the ground for roughly the past forty to fifty years. A new brick patio was also added in front of the Old Kitchen.

reconstruction. Incidentally, seven years later, in November 1965, another large but less significant fire started when a broiler in the kitchen caught fire. The flames went up through the ductwork to the second floor and roof. This fire damaged the roof and walls in some parts of the building, but repairs were made quickly.

During the restoration period in 1957, members of the Ford family retired as trustees of the inn. Elected to replace them were members of the National Trust for Historic Preservation. In 1960, the National Trust members retired and were replaced by members of local preservation committees and by local prominent business, civic and academic leaders. This twelve-person board continues today to administer the nonprofit Wayside Inn Trust (which owns, on behalf of the public, the inn) and the Wayside Inn Corporation (the entity that operates the inn under the trust).

Just after the restoration in 1958, the fourth inn manager under the trust took over the inn's operation. The business, however, was reportedly losing $20,000 a month, so something had to change. The trustees, hoping to make the inn run more profitably, hired Frank Koppeis as "innkeeper" after thirty-five years of having a "manager" under Ford and the early trust. "Mr. K" had a background in hotel service, a sense of thrift and the right personality to bring back the meaning of "hospitality" to the inn. Frank ran the inn from March 1959 to November 1989. He was just the right person, at the right time, for the inn.

FRANK KOPPEIS, THE TRUST'S FIRST INNKEEPER

For thirty years, Frank Koppeis was the face and heart of the inn. Frank was a pilot in the U.S. Air Force and served in World War II. After spending eleven years in the military, he joined the management of a large suburban Boston hotel. He quickly picked up hotel service skills and was soon recommended for the head position at the inn when it became available. Frank sought to build strong relationships with the local community, the staff and his guests at the inn. He wanted to make a dinner or stay at the inn memorable for all. Often he would dress in colonial garb and recite the tale of the How family and the inn. Frank was particularly fond of the garden, and during his tenure, the roses and other plantings were meticulously maintained. He also ceremoniously planted a tree every year.

Frank sought to bring back the colonial spirit of the inn, particularly with the bicentennial coming in the not-too-distant future. In 1964, under his auspices, he helped organize the Sudbury Companies of Militia and Minute, as well as the Sudbury Ancient Fyfe and Drum Companie. The annual "12 mile march" on April 19, reenacting the Sudbury Militia's 1775 march to Concord's Old North Bridge, was begun by Frank—a tradition that continues on today. Frank also introduced the Coow Woow (rum and ginger brandy) and Stone Wall (gin and apple jack), two colonial-rooted cocktails still popular at the inn. One important facilities project, for which Frank labored sixteen years to get accomplished, was to bury the utility lines in front of the inn. This finally occurred in late 1989–90, just after he retired. This was a new look after roughly 104 years of seeing the wires overhead.

After the inn was beautifully restored in 1958, there was a desire to keep it in pristine condition. At first, the Old Kitchen was made into a gift stop. Later, a gate was put across the Old Kitchen so visitors could only look into that space. You could enter the Bar Room, but there was no service, and you had to be careful not to touch the museum furniture. Frank changed all this over time, making the inn much more welcoming and comfortable. The inn also originally employed tour guides who continued the tradition of inn tours, but the fifty-cent fee was not enough to justify the cost of this service, so it eventually ended. Frank then let people wander through the inn, but pilfering became a problem, so he set up gates in front of the four museum rooms and fastened down everything else. Frank served the inn with all his heart for many years, and his influence still shows more than twenty years later.

Modern-Day Changes, Management and the Historic Mission

A significant renovation took place in 1999–2000, changing the front desk and gift shop area. An elevator, an innkeeper's office, downstairs bathrooms, a historic artifacts display and an underground stair connection to the basement kitchen from the Ford Room waitress area were all added. For the first time since the Ford era, the footprint of the inn changed. Approximately 3,220 square feet of new construction was added, and 2,440 square feet was renovated.

FLIP

Alice Morse Earle tells us in her classic book *Stagecoach and Tavern Days* (written in 1900):

> *Flip was made in a great pewter mug or earthen pitcher filled two-thirds full of strong; beer; sweetened with sugar, molasses, or dried pumpkin, according to individual taste or capabilities; and flavored with "a dash"—about a gill—of New England rum. Into this mixture was thrust and stirred a red-hot loggerhead, made of iron and shaped like a poker, and the seething iron made the liquor foam and bubble and mantle high, and gave it the burnt, bitter taste so dearly loved.*
>
> *Many a reader…inspired by the picture, has heated an iron poker or flip-dog and brewed and drunk a mug of flip. I did so not long ago, mixing carefully by a rule for flip recommended and recorded and used by General Putnam—Old Put— in the Revolution. I had the Revolutionary receipt and I had the Revolutionary loggerhead, and I had the old-time ingredients, but alas, I had neither the tastes nor the digestion of my Revolutionary sires, and the indescribable scorched and puckering bitterness of taste and pungency of smell of that rank compound which was flip, will serve for some time in my memory as an antidote for any overweening longing for the good old times.*

Frank Koppeis in the 1960s holding a loggerhead and making the colonial drink "flip" in front of the west fireplace in the Taproom (then the main socializing area).

A few years later, in 2005, the board of trustees hired a planning/architectural firm to help develop a master strategic plan for the business. Several recommendations came out of this; an easy one was to "refresh" the inn to make it a bit more attractive. The inn hired a local decorating company in 2009 to add new curtains, stencils and accessories throughout and new carpeting in the Ford Room and ballroom (changing for the first time ever its function as a dance hall).

Another recommendation in the master plan was to restore and repurpose the barn across the street, a project in the planning stages. A third recommendation was to improve the facilities for weddings, which the inn has done wonderfully. To help with the wedding business, a three-season white wedding tent has been added just east of the Longfellow garden/parking area. The chapel was refreshed by exposing and refinishing the original hardwood floor, adding new seat cushions and putting on some fresh paint. To support the growing hotel and wedding business, the inn secured a long-term lease on an adjacent hotel property (one mile east) and began operation of the Wayside Inn Carriage House in June 2010. The ten rooms at the inn were never enough for wedding travelers and other guests; it now has forty-six more.

Another recommendation was to provide some outdoor dining space (Lemon and Ford both had an outside screened porch, but this was not put back after the fire). In June 2011, a new brick and granite patio was opened just outside the Old Dining Room door. Along with it, a matching front walkway was added. John Cowden, the innkeeper since 2009, has overseen all these recent changes.

The inn's mission to preserve and present its history to the public is accomplished foremost by keeping it well maintained and accessible to public. Underlying this is efficient business management, so the inn is self-sustaining. The mission is also achieved by fostering cultural activities. A successful antique show is held in May, as is a "Woolly Days" sheep-shearing event. A series of "Summer Strawberry Concerts" run throughout July at the chapel, and other music concerts are held elsewhere on site throughout the year. The militia performs door duty every weekend. The fife and drums perform every Wednesday evening from April through September. A large colonial fair (started by Frank Koppeis) is held every year on the last Saturday in September (this year marks the fortieth anniversary of that event). A large and very entertaining battle reenactment is held in October. Formal colonial balls open to the public are held three times a year. An eighteenth-century dance troupe started by the current itinerant dancemaster Al Petty has been active at the inn since 2008. Ice harvesting is done in February, and the grist-milling operations are run daily throughout the year.

11

THE OLD BAR ROOM
The Heart of the Inn

Where dozed a fire of beechen logs
that bred Strange fancies in its embers golden dred,
And nursed the loggerhead,
whose hissing dip,
timed by wise instinct,
creamed the bowl of flip.
—James Lowell, 1868

Few rooms in the inn hold as many memories as the old Bar Room. They still linger about, even after the reconstruction work required over fifty years ago. Passing over the room's threshold have been Samuel and David, the many Patriots and soldiers, Ezekiel, Portsmouth, Adam, Jerusha, Lyman, Aunt Margey, the Puffers, the Dadmuns, the Seymours, Howe, Rogers, Lemon, Ford, Koppeis and all their loved ones. Countless transient visitors have entered. Here, too, passed Hawthorne, Emerson, Thoreau, Longfellow and five characters in Longfellow's poem. (While the Parlor across the hall is where the fictitious characters of Longfellow were placed, you would almost think the real people on whom he based the characters walked over to the Bar Room to relax for the evening.)

We turn to a few reminiscences of the old Bar Room held in the archives to try to bring back a sense of what it must have been like in days past.

Hudson writes of this room in its early days:

> *Here in…the old Bar Room nightly sat the miscellaneous groups made up of teamsters, horse-jockeys, traveling agents, itinerant showmen, cattle-drivers, peddlers, or mysterious strangers. The discussions that arose, the stories told, the jokes that were cracked, as the foaming flip went round, have never been placed on record. Forsooth, "A jolly place in times of old."*

Adeline Lunt gives us an amusing look at Lyman in this room, in the early to mid-1800s:

> *The Squire was very much afraid of lightning—so much so that during the continuance of any very violent thunder-storms he had the habit of securing what he considered the safest position by placing his chair in the very centre of the Bar Room, between two well-polished nails that protruded to the surface. Here, with his feet up on the rounds of the chair, he counted and calculated the distance and the danger of every successive flash and report. On one particular occasion, when the thunder was roaring and the lightning flashing, he was found sitting in the dark in a small passageway that separated the Bar Room from the clock-room, so called. Aunt Margey herself uneasy from the violence of the storm, in wandering from her kitchen corner, found the Squire in his retreat. Putting up the finger, she ejaculated, "H-a-a! y-o-u c-a-n-'t g-e-t a-w-a-y f-r-o-m t-h-e w-r-a-a-t-h o-f God."*

The *Boston Traveler*, on July 19, 1865, gives us another early account:

> *On entering the house, at the right is the Bar Room, now entirely deserted. Across the room at the furthest corner is the bar, enclosing the desk and store-room; the black and smoky rafters and the worn and sunken floor give evidence that in the old time this room at least, was rarely wanting of occupants.*

Drake gives us a more physical description for the 1870 period:

> *Everything remains as of old. There is the bar in one corner of the common room, with its wooden portcullis, made to be hoisted or let down at pleasure, but over which never appeared that ominous announcement, "No liquors sold over this bar." The little desk where the tipplers' score was set down,*

and the old escritoire, looking as if it might have come from some hospital for decayed and battered furniture, are there now. The bare floor, which once received its regular morning sprinkling of clean white sea-sand, the bare beams and timbers overhead, from which the whitewash has fallen in flakes, and the very oak of which is seasoned with the spicy vapors steaming from pewter flagons, all remind us of the good old days before the flood of new ideas. Governors, magistrates, generals, with scores of others whose names are remembered with honor, have been here to quaff a health or indulge in a drinking-bout.

When Lucie Welsh, the schoolteacher, had her parents visit in 1884, she recalls:

I remember my mother's surprising reaction to this room. She was a woman of well-balanced mind and natural poise. After a few minutes of conversation with Mrs. Dadmun, she said, "I think we should be starting back now," and walked to the door. "But father is not ready yet," I remonstrated. "He will come very soon, and I will wait outside for him," which she did, standing on the wide doorstone next to the pump. She told me later that she could not have stayed another minute in that dreary room.

Wallace Downes tells us in the *New England Magazine* of 1887:

The oak flooring of this room has been worn thinner than that of any other in the hostelry, by the tread of nearly two centuries. Across the ceiling the great beams are entirely blackened by steam rising from innumerable pots of "nut-brown liquor." There can be no doubt but that this was the best patronized place in the whole house.

On September 4, 1892, the *New York Tribune* wrote:

Over forty years ago this fall—what is now the most famous inn-company of America were sitting in the spacious but dingy Bar-kitchen of the old Red-Horse Tavern of Sudbury Mass. On the left of the big hall as you enter is the Inn parlor, and on the right the old barroom, now used as a kitchen. The barroom, although now made use of as a paltry modern kitchen, is eminently suggestive. What cannot a man with keen imagination picture to himself as he looks on this spacious low-ceilinged room with its great oak rafters blackened by the smoke of numberless pipes and modern

The Bar Room in the 1870s and '80s when it was a "paltry kitchen." The bar is being utilized as the kitchen storeroom.

cigars etc…On the great central rafter, which runs east and west, are hooks on which hams were hung—with the exception of one much larger than the rest. On this great iron staple were thrown the chains of a prisoner, whenever a constable had one in his charge and had occasion to stop for refreshments.

The *New York Times*, on November 20, 1897, speaks similarly about the old beams overhead, then mentions the green wainscoting and

over the mantelpiece hang an old musket and swords, and a curious little wooden canteen. On the wall nearby are some old lanterns and one or two old prints…One of the most interesting items in this room is Paul Revere's engraving of old Boston. Over a large and curiously carved desk at one side is an oil painting of the last landlord, Lyman How. The other works of art in this room include several silhouette portraits, engravings of Lafayette and Lord Chesterfield, old prints of the Boston Massacre, and one or two other battle scenes, and an eighteenth century allegory of the "High Horse

Champion and His Seconds." A huge old spinning wheel and antique safe, together with various splint-bottom chairs complete the furnishings of this thoroughly old-fashioned room.

An October 5, 1899 (early Lemon era) newspaper called the *Journal* of Southbridge, Massachusetts, tells us:

Here is the seat where the travelers dozed from a long ride. Here is the old flip iron, money till, two Leyden Schnapps jars, here is the broad awl that drew all the corks of the bottles. When not in use it hung on the wall and a hole made in the panel tells how long it has been hung there. But now from the ancient portcullis are served only "Bill's sparking tonic," ginger, soda, etc. From this room leads a steep stair case where were beds for drivers, slaves, and common folk.

For almost 200 years this old kitchen which they sat had been the center of revelry and good cheers whenever the position of the Boston mail coach curtly shouted, "The Red Horse—stop fifteen minutes!" or whenever a belated rider tossed his reins into the hands of a waiting stableman, strode

The Bar Room in 1897 (early Lemon era). Note the lace-lined shelves, "Sudbury" brand cigars, wallpaper, fireplace insert and "Bill's Tonic" sign mentioned in the 1899 article.

The Bar Room in 1908 (later Lemon era). He took the wallpaper down but left the fireplace insert. No alcohol was served; this was a lounge. He served tea in this room.

The Bar Room in the 1940s Ford era. You can see the sap bucket hanging on wall and the bar used as a front office and gift shop (room keys hang on the wall). Atherton Roger's safe is under the tippler's desk.

into the mist of the cheery company indoors, and answered all questions about the progress of the war and the movements of the Redcoats, as he sipped his mug of ale with increasing good spirits.

LEMON ERA

Sudbury was a dry town during the Lemon era.[66] Bringing alcohol back was on the town ballot year after year, but it was always defeated. Lemon used this room as a lounge and to serve tea. In Ford's time (1923–45), he simply had a firm no alcohol policy. The bar for both eras served as the inn desk, as well as the gift shop. One relic over the fireplace was a Revolutionary musket, carried by a Sudbury man, Ephraim Smith. He was loaned this gun by the town authorities for the April 19 fight. The receipt promising a safe return of the gun was signed by Smith on April 17, 1775, and for a long time it was preserved in this room. Unfortunately, it did not survive the fire (copies were made, though). The gun survived, but it was stolen in the 1980s. The musket now hanging was donated by Milt Swanson and is said to have been made by Waters and possibly used in the War of 1812.

FORD ERA

One of the artifacts Ford had hanging in this room was the "old Coolidge sap bucket." Back in 1924, Republican President Coolidge invited Ford, Edison and Harvey Firestone to his father's house in Plymouth, Vermont, to hopefully gain support from the outspoken democrat Ford and the others in the upcoming

Colonel John Coolidge, Mrs. Coolidge, Thomas Edison, Harvey Firestone Jr., Henry Ford, President Coolidge and Harvey Firestone signing the famous sap bucket, August 1924.

Damage to the bar from the 1955 fire.

The Bar Room in 1958, right after the restoration. The pristine edge eventually came off, but it remained this way until the early 1990s, when the Bar Room was finally reopened for service. It has since become warm and inviting. Ford acquired the square table in the middle of the room from a local antiques dealer. It is said to date from 1675 and is still in use.

presidential election. The bucket, circa 1780, was made and used by Coolidge's "grandfather's grandfather," John Coolidge, one of the original settlers of this Vermont town. It was almost a priceless family heirloom. The August 20, 1924 *Boston Herald* records that Coolidge told Ford, "I thought perhaps you would like it to take back to the Wayside Inn in Sudbury." The whole party signed the bottom (as did Prince Edward of Wales, later, when he visited Ford in Detroit). Ford displayed it with honor in the Bar Room. You can see it hung just to the right of the bar. It survives at the inn but is not displayed.

THE MODERN-ERA BAR

Alcohol came back to the inn in 1953, when the inn manager reapplied for a license. The bar in any restaurant is usually the largest income producer, and the inn at that time was struggling. It needed this new income source, and not having bar service was a competitive disadvantage. People wanted drinks (and cigarettes) with their meals. The first modern-era bar was in what is now the Ford Room. This room even had a separate entrance with a sign outside calling it the Red Horse Room. The bar service was through the

THE RED HORSE ROOM: Formerly the 1800 Dining Room provides 'drink' of the old days as well as todays favorites.

From a 1960s-era brochure. Now called the Taproom, this room served as the bar from the 1960s through the early 1990s. Note the bar on the right of the picture.

Dutch door in this room and through the inside shuttered window (it is now a service area for the waitstaff). Since this wing did not get touched by the fire, the Red Horse Room opened back up even before the full inn did. At some point early in his tenure, Frank Koppeis moved the bar from the Ford Room across the tavern into what is now the Taproom. The Taproom remained the bar for the inn all the way into the early 1990s. In Frank's time, the Taproom was the center of the inn's activity.

During this period, the "Old Bar," as Frank called it, was used for people waiting for dinner. There was no service. The room contained several museum objects that could not be touched. In 1992, Bob Purrington, the next innkeeper from 1989 to 2009, turned the Bar Room into an actual active working bar, making it once again the true heart of the inn. The Taproom was turned into a quiet dining space.

Today's Bar Room

The mugs seen hanging from the rafters today belong to the past colonels of the reorganized Sudbury Militia Company (since 1964). The fireplace is the only working fireplace in the inn; the others are gas (another Purrington-era change. Understandably, the risk of another fire was just too great). Above the fireplace, Frank Koppeis proudly hung one of the more interesting pieces of original art at the inn. Russ Kirby, a local Sudbury master woodworker and member of the fife and drum group, created a set of twenty-six matching fifes, known as the Red Horse Fifes, out of the Wayside Inn's own timbers back in 1971. The one hanging is the first of the set and is made of chestnut. The fife set is played on special occasions around the inn. The black and gold Wayside Inn sign hanging in this room was given to Henry Ford in 1926. It was reportedly stolen from the inn twenty years earlier by a group of Harvard students having fun. These students left it in a sleigh rented to them by a Wellesley Hills farmer named William Diehl. Diehl wrote to Ford that he had the "sign that hung over the front door" and that Diehl wanted to give it to the inn. Ford went out to Diehl's farm to gratefully accept it.

The Old Bar of the Early How Period
(the Original Taproom)

Inside the Bar Room stands the railed bar. While very old, the original bar—or "Taproom," as it was called—was likely the small room right behind it. This small Taproom could serve both the Bar Room and the Old Dining Room by raising its small flap doors. Now, it nicely hides a refrigerator and beer tap for the modern bar. This little room caught the attention of many nineteenth- and twentieth-century writers. Charles Lawrence wrote a typical description for the *Boston Sunday Globe Magazine* in 1923:

The Old Bar Room

Inside the original Taproom looking into the Bar Room. Note the holes in the door from the awl, used as a bottle opener for it seems many generations.

A half-hidden door leads back of the bar, and through its lattice the tapster could talk unseen with the barmaid...In this little passage room the liquors were uncorked with a common awl, which was then stuck up against the closet doors...In time this so honeycombed them as to form an almost regular pattern...In one place there is a hole three inches in length by nearly that across.

It is not recorded when the railed bar outside the small original Taproom was originally installed. The only small bit of evidence available is an August 13, 1868 *Boston Journal* article that mentions, "As you enter the house, the high gate extending across the hall 'to keep the dogs away' will first meet your eyes; then enter the 'Bar Room' how old no one knows, nearby is the '<u>new bar</u>' where we see 'Uncle Adam' dispenses his mug of toddy." If this is referring to the railed bar in this room, it may indicate that Adam Howe was responsible for this addition to the room.

A HISTORY OF LONGFELLOW'S WAYSIDE INN

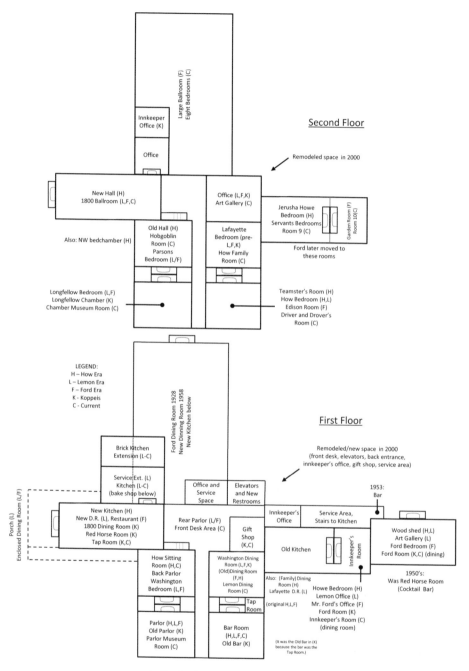

Second Floor

Innkeeper Office (K)

Large Ballroom (F)
Eight Bedrooms (C)

Office

Remodeled space in 2000

New Hall (H)
1800 Ballroom (L,F,C)

Office (L,F,K)
Art Gallery (C)

Jerusha Howe Bedroom (H)
Servants Bedrooms Room 9 (C)

Garden Room (F)
Room 10 (C)

Also: NW bedchamber (H)

Old Hall (H)
Hobgoblin Room (C)
Parsons Bedroom (L/F)

Lafayette Bedroom (pre-L,F,K)
How Family Room (C)

Ford later moved to these rooms

Longfellow Bedroom (L,F)
Longfellow Chamber (K)
Chamber Museum Room (C)

Teamster's Room (H)
How Bedroom (H,L)
Edison Room (F)
Driver and Drover's Room (C)

LEGEND:
H – How Era
L – Lemon Era
F – Ford Era
K - Koppeis
C - Current

First Floor

Ford Dining Room 1928
New Dinning Room 1958
New Kitchen below

Brick Kitchen Extension (L-C)

Remodeled/new space in 2000
(front desk, elevators, back entrance, innkeeper's office, gift shop, service area)

Service Ext. (L)
Kitchen (L-C)
(bake shop below)

Office and Service Space

Elevators and New Restrooms

1953: Bar

Porch (L)
Enclosed Dining Room (L/F)

New Kitchen (H)
New D.R. (L), Restaurant (F)
1800 Dining Room (K)
Red Horse Room (K)
Tap Room (K,C)

Rear Parlor (L/F)
Front Desk Area (C)

Gift Shop (K,C)

Innkeeper's Office

Service Area, Stairs to Kitchen

Innkeeper's Room

Wood shed (H,L)
Art Gallery (L)
Ford Bedroom (F)
Ford Room (K,C) (dining)

Old Kitchen

How Sitting Room (H,C)
Back Parlor
Washington Bedroom (L,F)

Washington Dining Room (L,F,K)
(Old)Dining Room (F,H)
Lemon Dining Room (C)

Also: (Family) Dining Room (H)
Lafayette D.R. (L)
(original H,L,F)

Howe Bedroom (H)
Lemon Office (L)
Mr. Ford's Office (F)
Ford Room (K)
Innkeeper's Room (C)
(dining room)

1950's:
Was Red Horse Room
(Cocktail Bar)

Tap Room

Parlor (H,L,F)
Old Parlor (K)
Parlor Museum Room (C)

Bar Room (H,L,F,C)
Old Bar (K)

(It was the Old Bar in (K)
because the bar was the
Tap Room.)

Indicative Room Layout
(Illustrative, not exact)

12

THE INN ITSELF

An Account of the Rooms, Buildings and Surroundings

As it is the commendation of a good huntsman to find game in a wide wood, so it is no imputation if he has not caught all.
—Plato

A few other interesting aspects of the inn not mentioned elsewhere are covered in this chapter. We will start with a look outside.

OAKS AND ELMS

The mighty oak and elm trees were often written about back when the larger ones flanking the approach road still existed. The large ancient oaks measured eighteen feet in circumference and spread their branches over a space of more than two hundred feet. The two most significant and most photographed were the famous Longfellow oak and the Lemon oak. The Longfellow (white) oak was just across from the coach house, on the inn-side of the stone wall (on the dirt driveway). The Lemon (red) oak was across Wayside Inn Road, near the eastern corner of the coach house. The Longfellow oak has no recorded story associated with it, and it is not clear when it came down (it was before 1959). Both trees were huge and had large cavities inside them. The Lemon oak was named, so the legend says, when E.R. Lemon got stuck in it for several hours before he finally managed to wiggle free.[67] This tree came down in April 1959. The stump still remains if you look along the stone wall. In Lemon's days, these trees were estimated to be between three and five hundred years old. They were standing here when Captains Wadsworth and Brocklebank passed this way from Marlborough to fight and die in the Sudbury Fight of 1676, when Tantamous's son signed the Indian deed over in 1684, when the inn was built in the early 1700s, when Washington passed through in 1775 and still almost a century later when Longfellow wrote of them in his *Tales*:

> *Through the ancient oaks o'erhead*
> *Mysterious voices moaned and fled.*

If you look closely at the last surviving large oak tree just across the driveway from the garden, you can see that this one is all wired up and filled with concrete. This tree has no known history, but it is often captured in photos and paintings.

Children in the Longfellow oak, 1899 or 1900. Just behind it, across Wayside Inn Road, is the Lemon oak, which has a similar cavity. Vagrants would occasionally sleep in these. These were a significant part of the site for two to three hundred years; now, any memory of them is nearly gone.

On the western side of the inn, there were several notable elm trees. One, just beyond the house, had a twenty-foot circumference and massive roots protruding out of the ground on which people used to sit. On the opposite side of the road was another, slightly smaller elm that arched into this one, forming a connected canopy. According to Lunt, lightning struck "the" noble tree (presumably the larger one) and "somewhat damaged" it. This tree appears to be the one from which the original signboard was hung.

GARDEN

E.R. Lemon began the Longfellow Garden in 1905 on top of the old vegetable garden. The Longfellow bust was installed in 1918. Here, one could find a place of peaceful meditation. Several innkeepers took especially good care of it. There were beautiful gardens in the early Lemon, Ford and the Koppeis eras.

The Longfellow garden looking east at the Longfellow bust, Ford era. This garden was meant to help inspire artists coming to the inn.

SURROUNDINGS

Lunt tells us:

The ride over of about a mile and a half along a country road, through sweet-scented woods and bush, and upon high land with off-spreading pastoral landscapes, was exhilarating. A final turn brought us on the highway, in the old days the traveled thoroughfare between eastern and western Massachusetts, but now indeed a "region of repose"; and off to the left the Inn first appeared to our view in its picturesque setting, "just as Longfellow sketched it…A place of slumber and of dreams, Remote among the wooded hills."

She continues:

Indeed, the place with its surroundings—the whole lay of the land about it—was a little nook of peace and natural beauty. The pastoral picture, warmed into attractiveness by its varied aspects of meadow, woodland, hill, and valley, was intersected by a running brook of romantic winding. Although just before the approach to the house, or beyond, the landscape was of no marked character, yet at this particular spot nature seemed to have lavished careless beauty enough to make the place thoroughly charming and inviting. There was a natural welcome and air of hospitality about it in keeping with the place.

The drives about the place were in all directions very agreeable, and a great part of every fine day was spent in the pursuit. At no great distance from the house one might drive for miles through most enchanting woods, leading to Peacham [Peakham] Plains, so called—wild tracts of sandy, uncultivated land. White Pond, deriving its name from its white sandy bottom and beach like borders, almost entirely surrounded by dense woods, was a resort of extraordinary beauty. The old mill (and is ever a country picture perfect without one?), ruinous and romantic, was yet near enough to the house to make it a favorite stroll for moon-lit evenings or sunset sittings. Then there was this wonderful rock, where, led across open fields and woodland paths, one finally came to an almost circular opening, which revealed this colossal and enormous boulder. This was a favorite Sunday forenoon stroll with the Professor and his little coterie, where, seated on the mossy turf, they were wont to find there sermons, as well as good in everything.

Red Horse Spring

Just beside the barn is a low A-frame structure. This houses the old wellhead for what once was a spring. Lemon advertised this in a brochure for the inn, stating, "The water used at the Inn is from the Red Horse spring, one of the finest sources of drinking water in the State." The spring went dry after 1927; it is suspected that the blasting done for the Route 20 bypass road may have altered the water table. The structure is currently used for storage.

Stone Bridge and Roads

A report in the archives states that the old stone bridge built over Hop Brook just west of the inn may have been put in after 1823, when the "feather and pin" method of construction was introduced. No one really knows when it was built, but it seems older than this date. When the state moved the road in 1899, a new stone and steel bridge was constructed several yards away from the original. This bridge had a beam on it marked 1904, so it seems the bridge went up at the end of the project. Longfellow, in his

The old stone bridge looking north, mid- to late 1800s.

Tales, writes of the young Sicilian watching over the sides of the old bridge:

> *And, leaning o'er the bridge of stone,*
> *To watch the speckled trout glide by,*
> *And float through the inverted sky.*

Barns

While there is only one barn on the site now, there used to be several. What happened to them and what they were used for is a mystery, as is the exact age of the current barn (although we have a clue for this one; on one of the top plates in the southeast corner, the date "1825" is written). The few reminiscences to draw from lead to more confusion. Atherton Rogers mentions that during the 1893–97 period, they "changed the old driveway barn so the hill in front of the house might be seen." Which barn they moved is not entirely clear. They possibly moved the large James Puffer barn (what happened to it is unknown),[68] or more likely they moved another horse barn that both Newcomb and Seymour mention in their comments to Ford. Both refer to a barn that was on the original site of the coach house near the garden.

Lemon's carpenter Newcomb notes, "Barn now located at the corner of the Wayside Inn and Post Roads was moved from the side of the present coach house in 1895…the Barn was located on the old coach house site." (The Wayside Inn Road at that time was the dirt road to Framingham, not the paved road in front.)

Seymour's notes to Ford on what happened during the Lemon period state, "Barn now located across state road formerly occupied site near where Coach House now stands, was moved by State when road was changed. Barn which was burned had been moved from site directly in front of Inn and was known as the Cow barn."

Clifton Church, a noted black-and-white photographer, took at least two series of photographs of the inn sometime in the 1915–18 time period. One

The current barn in 1923, late Lemon era, before Ford's restoration. Note the fairly well-used road to Framingham running next to it (then called the Wayside Inn Road).

contains a rare picture of a barn that looks to be just east of the inn near the garden. It may have been the second barn that was moved (possibly the Puffer barn), which later burned.

William Parmenter, who lived at the inn as a child during Lyman's time, commented (to Ford), "The Inn and surrounding buildings have been changed considerably since he lived there. He recalls a horse barn large enough to accommodate 100 horses, this was located a short distance up Wayside Inn Road on the easterly side."

There is also the following comment of a lightning strike in August 1868 (from a farmers' journal newspaper whose name was not preserved):

The shed part of the old "Red Horse" tavern…was struck by lightning and consumed, with two tons of hay and some farming equipment. The main building was fortunately saved unharmed. The lightning struck first one of the large oak trees in the famous row which shade the road by the inn, and then passed by means of an iron rod from the tree to the shed, setting it on fire. Many years ago the shed, probably a century old or more, showed signs of toppling over, and this iron rod was put in to be stiffened by the great "oak."

WAYSIDE INN RAILROAD STATION

According to the book *1639–1939, A Brief History of Sudbury from Its Beginnings* by the Federal Writers' Project, the first railroad line in town came in 1871 (a north–south line). In 1881, the Massachusetts Central line built the east–west route. (Even though these trains came late to Sudbury, Lyman's business in the 1850s would be impacted by trains bypassing Sudbury altogether.) In addition to the stations in Sudbury, there was a small station out in the woods on Dutton Road for the Wayside Inn. Passengers would need to flag down a train, as this was not a scheduled stop. Ford, Lemon, Babe Ruth and thousands of guests would depart from this station. The station was roughly a mile and a half from the inn and was burned down by vandals in the 1940s.

In a February 10, 1887 *Christian Union* newspaper article by Margaret Wright called "The Wayside Inn," we read that it was "nothing more than a weather beaten platform besides a sandy cart-path running through the pine wood." She describes an isolated ride through the woods, eventually coming up on the western side of the inn and riding over the stone bridge. Hudson tells us in 1889, "The Massachusetts Central Railroad runs through it [Peakham], and has a station called the 'Wayside Inn Station.' The situation

The Wayside Inn railroad waiting room was built by the Boston & Maine Railroad in 1897. Looking north up Dutton Road. *Courtesy of Robert Seymour and the Sudbury Historical Society.*

of this depot is exceptionally secluded, no other building being in sight on account of the woods by which it is nearly surrounded." By 1897, it seems the station had been updated.

STRUCTURE

Menders, Torrey & Spencer, the architectural consultant firm hired to help with the master plan in 2005, describes the inn architecture:

> *The Inn represents an evolution of simple forms and massing that have been created to respond to changing needs and tastes over three centuries. It is the design of house wrights and joiners. It can be described as vernacular architecture—which is to say that it was not designed by an architect or individual with formal training, but represents a craft and building tradition that is typical to its locale.*

The Inn Itself

Charlotte Whitcomb, writing in *The Book of a Hundred Houses* (1902), tells us:

> *The house is a good specimen of early colonial architecture. It is not disguised by modern alterations in any essential feature, but bears its credentials on its face. Built upon honor, the storms of two hundred and odd New England winters have searched every cranny of the old hostelry, whistled down the big chimneystacks, raved around the gables of the gambrel roof, and departed, always valiantly withstood by the integrity of the handiwork of the colonial craftsmen.*

INSIDE THE TAVERN

Parlor

To the left as you enter the inn is the Parlor. Long ago this was the "best" room for guests, particularly for women not entering the Bar Room. Longfellow uses this room as the *mise en scène* of the *Tales*. He sets the tone beautifully:

> *The fire-light, shedding o'er all*
> *The splendor of its ruddy glow,*
> *Filled the whole parlor, large and low;*

The Parlor in the Ford period, showing the Lemon/Ford collection of Longfellow items.

Later, he goes on to itemize the relics he sees and mentions Jerusha's pianoforte. Today, only the coat of arms and the somber clock remain in this room. The sword and Molineaux glass are on display in the new artifact case near the back entrance. During the fire, many of the artifacts in this room were covered with a thick coat of ice and amazingly were preserved. The glass picture of Princess Mary fell off the wall and shattered—that was one loss. The mantel was destroyed, too. The mantel you see today is a replica of the one seen in the opening etching of the *Tales* (the first edition).

The Parlor had its dark days. In the 1892 *New York Tribune*, we read, "If contrasts are to be dwelt upon, then should the present aspect of the old reception room just across the hall from the barroom be deprecated. For, outside of a table and two dilapidated chairs, nothing decks this once garishly decorated chamber." A July 19, 1865 *Boston Journal* article notes that in some places the floor has sunk nearly a half foot and that Jerusha Howe's handmade carpet was still on the floor.

The pianoforte, the first in Sudbury, was made by Babcock of Boston. After Lyman's death, the inn's furnishings were auctioned, and the pianoforte was sold. Henry Ford's agents found it in an estate sale in Weston. Ford had it sent to Dearborn for restoration, and then it was placed back in the Parlor in 1940. It was damaged in the fire fifteen years later, but Frank Koppeis had it restored in 1960 with restoration funds sent in by donors.

1774 Windowpanes

During Ezekiel's ownership, the famous William Molineaux Jr. windowpanes were presumably etched with a diamond ring in the Parlor (June 24, 1774). One had a brief poem and the other the signature. The poem read:

> *What do you think?*
> *Here is good drink,–*
> *Perhaps you may not know it.*
> *If not in haste, do stop and taste,*
> *You merry folks will show it.*
>
> *Wm. Molineaux, Jr., Esq.,*
> *24 June, 1774, Boston*

The first mention of these panes actually existing is in a note from Longfellow to Miss Eaton, who showed Longfellow the inn when he visited in 1862. He sent her a thank-you note and had a further request: "Speaking

The Inn Itself

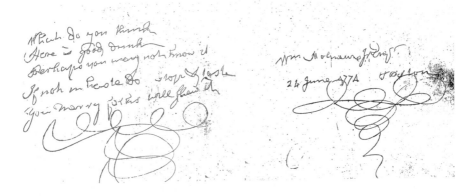

The two famous Molineaux window etchings.

of the old inn he [Professor Treadwell] said that on one of the parlor window panes were written some verses, with a date. Would you be so kind as to copy them for me or any names and dates written on the windows?" How they missed these on a tour is a mystery; nevertheless, she copied them and sent them off. A few days later, the Prelude to the *Tales of a Wayside Inn*, containing a reference to Molineaux's verse, was written:

> *And, flashing on the window-pane,*
> *Emblazoned with its light and shade*
> *The jovial rhymes, that still remain,*
> *Writ near a century ago,*
> *By the great Major Molineaux,*
> *Whom Hawthorne has immortal made.*

Nathaniel Hawthorne, upon reading that his friend honored him by putting his name in the poem, sent a note to Longfellow:

> *Concord, January 2, 1864. Dear Longfellow,—It seems idle to tell you that I have read the* Wayside Inn *with great comfort and delight. I take vast satisfaction in your poetry, and take very little in most other men's, except it be the grand old strains that have been sounding on through all my life…It gratifies my mind to find my own name shining in your verse—even as if I had been gazing up at the moon and detected my own features in its profile…*

Some poetic license was clearly taken here. Longfellow's and Hawthorne's Molineaux seem like separate characters, and neither is as Longfellow claimed. For one, in Hawthorne's 1852 story, "The Snow-Image, and Other Twice-Told Tales," the fictitious Major Molineux character gets tarred and feathered at the end—hardly a description for a "great" Patriot. The real William Molineux Jr. (d. 1819) was the *son* of a famous Patriot. William Sr. was in the political circles of the great Patriot politicians Adams and Otis, and he was a leader in the Tea Party (he was also said to have been poisoned). The Molyneux Genealogy mentions that William Jr. was a major who served in an independently formed Boston militia company, commanded by John Hancock, for twenty-one days in 1777 and that he marched from Boston to Rhode Island. There is no mention of any great deeds, and there are very few other details on him to be found—other than that he was apparently at the tavern. The father William Molineux appears to be the "great" Patriot of record, and he was neither a major nor a "Jr." With respect to the spellings, they must be interchangeable. It is also difficult to discern if the etching is "Molineux" or "Molineaux." Longfellow/Eaton say "Molineaux."

There are two references in the archives regarding which window in the Parlor they were specifically in. There is a September 9, 1867 *Evening Gazette* newspaper article that mentions that the panes written on were "in the window, nearest to the main hall door stoop." A second article by a student, Florence Whittemore, on July 19, 1865, states close to the same: "The window nearest the entrance has been celebrated for the jovial rhythms." By June 24, 1874 (the 100th anniversary), the panes had been removed from the windows. The poem pane was broken at some point in recent history, but it has been reassembled and is on display in the inn.

It is interesting that the poem is very similar to the poem at the head of the Ezekiel chapter written by the famous English poet William Shenstone. Shenstone's poem was also etched in a window in 1750, but this legend comes from the Red Lion Inn in Henley, England. It is a legend, as the pane no longer exists, and another tavern, the White Swan in Henley-on-Avon, claims to be the place the poem was first written—albeit not etched in glass. One wonders if the later poem attributed to Molineaux may have been inspired by the earlier one. In 1882, another Parlor window etching occurred. Childe Hassam, a noted painter, scratched his name in another of the panes. Much later in the tavern's life, Edsel Ford etched his and seven friends' names in the window of the Longfellow Bedroom in 1925 (likely destroyed in the fire because records of it no longer exist).

The Inn Itself

Attic/Slave Bunk

In an 1891 letter on a visit to the Wayside Inn by Mr. and Mrs. Rice Hugh, we read:

> *The garret had three rooms in it, one was used for storing corn above which tramps were allowed to sleep. It was reached by a ladder which was taken down after the people were turned in for the night. Next to this was a small room in which was a modern shelf. It looked much like a shelf sink, it was about five feet high and was reached by a broad ladder having only four rungs. This was said to have been occupied by a lame negro boy and he slept in this bunk. He died and was buried on the farm. On the opposite side was a room said to have been used as a prison.*

A *Boston Journal* article of August 11, 1868, provides another early tour of the attic:

> *In one corner it will be pointed out the "corn room," near this is the "slave's room" and at the other end of the house is "No.10" the only room in the house that has a number which is famous as being the place where those who were thought to be suspicious characters or unfit to lodge in the "traveler's room" were locked up for their night's repose.*

In the 1887 *New England Magazine*, Wallace Downes wrote:

> *Ascending another flight of crazy stairs brings us to the old attic, about which the spiders have strewn a great net-work of cobwebs. All about here were stretched beds innumerable, which were occupied by the very commonest lodgers.*

Slave bed in the attic, believed to be in the northwest corner. Drawn by noted landscape architect Arthur Shurtleff in 1891. This picture and others he drew, along with a letter, are hanging in the Innkeeper's Room.

One of four Lemon-era rooms added to the third floor. This room was the Ole Bull Room in the northeast corner. This dormer window is on the rear of the roofline.

There is an old room up here known as the "grain room," from the fact that during the Indian wars the grain was stored here to protect it from the savages. Places appear in the floor where great cracks have been covered with axe-hewn boards, pieces of old boot leather and cow-hide which never saw a tannery; and the walls are honeycombed with great holes, made by the rats.

Once Lemon restored the attic in 1897, Charles Lawrence tells us, "Rooms on the third floor are mainly occupied by the family of the landlord."

Basement

Seymour tells us that the "deep part near the furnace was used as a meat storage space and was one of two rooms in [the] cellar, the other being at the SW corner, part now used as emergency coal bin, and known as wine cellar." This second space is the room under the Parlor. It is also mentioned as the "wine room" in a July 7, 1898 lawsuit document from *Jones v. Lemon*. It is mentioned as the "rum cellar" in the Forbes book of an earlier time.

Charles Loring, in an article in the 1926 *Garden and Home Magazine*, tells us, "There is also the 'deep hole' [in the basement]…the primitive, cold storage room, excavated three-four feet below the floor of the rest of the cellar and heavily walled with stone." (This is probably the first space Seymour mentions.)

Today, the basement under the Parlor and Bar Room is the maintenance shop. Under the Old Dining Room and Washington Bedroom/dining room is the break area for employees. The entire area under the north wing is the modern kitchen. The bakeshop is under the first-floor service kitchen; below the Taproom is the bakeshop's storage area. The east wing under the Old Kitchen and Ford Room is for non-food storage. Ductwork, sprinkler pipes, conduits and HVAC equipment also fill a good part of basement. You cannot really see any old remnants of the past. The stone walls are coated white.

Hobgoblin Room

The Old Hall (as it was originally called) in the upstairs northwest corner of the house was presumably used in Ezekiel's time to hold dancing parties and large group meetings. It proved too small, and the larger, attached New Hall was built sometime in the late Ezekiel period. Ezekiel's will points to the Old Hall as a bedchamber, which quite possibly was his own. In Lemon's days, the Old Hall was converted into a bedroom called the Parsons Bedroom (after T.W. Parsons, the poet of the *Tales*).

In 1868, it was first called the Hobgoblin Room. The story goes (according to old hostess notes) that "a woman of the Howe family [long ago] claimed she saw a ghost half floating, half running through this room on a dark night."

In the closet of the Old Hall were kept the archives of the Wayside Inn. Somehow they managed to be saved before the fire tore through this room. (Old records were also kept in the Parlor closet, in the closet under the stairs to the ballroom and under the bed in the Lafayette Room.)

In the Dadmun time, the Old Hall was turned into spare sleeping space for the hired men in the neighborhood. When rebuilt in 1958, it went back to its original function as a small hall. Today, this room is still called the Hobgoblin Room.

The Old Hall or Hobgoblin Room with the Lemon-era conversion into the Parsons Bedroom. This room may have been Ezekiel's bedroom. It is still kept open today as a dance hall.

1800 Ballroom

Once called the New Hall, this is the room of music and memories. Countless dances, balls and other social gatherings have been held over the years. Old records tell us of sleigh riding parties coming to the inn and holding dances in this ballroom, even during the tenant period when the inn did not operate. An 1871 reminiscence talks of cleaning up the room, and because the floor was so worn, they had to drive the nails down and plane the floor. It mentions dances started again, but they became so popular that they had to shut them down (presumably the crowds grew too large to support).

Ezekiel's will first mentions this room in 1796, calling it a new "long chamber." Typically, chamber means bedroom, so it likely was not a ballroom when first built. Adam was thought to have fitted it out later for dancing.

Whitcomb, in the 1899 *House Beautiful* magazine, tells us:

> *In the ball-room the floor is worn to satin smoothness by friction with many generations of flying feet. A large-patterned paper covers the walls. It was put on in squares, as was the mode before rolls came in. Lanthorns are suspended as a means of illumination; a railed dais at*

The 1800 Ballroom (or New Hall) seen during the Lemon era. The musicians' stand is to the rear left. The black ceiling is to hide unsightly soot from candles or, in this case, oil lanterns. This room is filled with memories like the barroom.

one end accommodates the fiddlers, and benches with hinged lids are fastened to the walls; the box-seats under the lids were thus made to give place to the fair ones' wraps.

The *New York Tribune* of 1892 tells us:

The [wall]*paper, what little of it is left to be seen, is also very old, bearing gaudy pictures of a good woman and two children sailing around in space in a cockleshell of a boat, a passable representation of Virtue. The paper in this room—as in the Washington and Lafayette rooms—is sadly desecrated by those autograph scourges, who insist on coupling their names with everything which savors of note. Almost every available space is scribbled with names, dating from 1866 to the current year* [1892]. *Here a bridal couple left their signatures, artistically blended with a heart; there you see the thirty-odd names of a sleigh-ride party, who visited the old Wayside Inn some ten years ago and enjoyed a merry dance in the historic hall.*

A February 17, 1924 *Detroit Free Press* newspaper article covering the private grand opening party Ford held mentions a conversation Ford had with Longfellow's youngest daughter, Anne (Longfellow) Thorpe (1855–1934). Anne, a dance enthusiast, told Ford that the spring of the old dance hall was not "as springy as it used to be." Ford had reinforced the floor supports earlier because he was concerned about the floor's age. He didn't mention this to Anne, but he did tell her he was "going to put springs under the girders." It's unknown if this ever happened. Four years later, Ford built a new dance hall (the second floor of the north wing) and had car springs installed under the floor to give it some bounce. The 1800 Ballroom was completely destroyed in the fire. What you see now is a meticulously researched reconstruction of the old one.

Large Ballroom

Henry Ford constructed a very large ballroom over the new dining room in 1928. It was quite similar in design to the 1800 Ballroom. This room was specially designed with leaf-type automobile springs under the floorboards for better dance action. This wing was completely destroyed after the fire, and when rebuilt, eight new guest rooms were constructed in place of the open dance floor.

Ford's large ballroom over the north wing dining room. Edison's new phonograph is being used to play the music, and car springs are under the floor to give it spring. This hall burned down in 1955.

The Lemon-era Innkeeper's Room (then just called his office). Now it is stripped down to bare wood and used as a dining room.

The Inn Itself

Innkeeper's Room

Just off the Old Kitchen is a small dining room known as the Innkeeper's Room. Years ago, this served as E.R. Lemon's private office and later as Henry Ford's private office. In the How era, this was likely a How family bedroom. Both *Arts and Decoration Magazine* in October 1916 and the 1923 Lawrence *Boston Globe* article mention this as the Squire Howe Bedroom. This makes sense, as his sister was upstairs, and this was probably the warmest section of the house. Lunt somewhat confirms the location by telling us, "The Squire and his servants occupied a portion somewhat removed and the main body of the house was given up to the guest." If this was Lyman's bedroom, then this is where he passed away. It was just an open display room in the Koppeis era. In the 1990s, it became a small dining room.

Jerusha's Bedroom

Current Room #9 in the upstairs east wing was Jerusha Howe's bedroom. At the time, this space was described as three small rooms along a narrow hall. The current room next door (Room#10, which Ford called the Garden Room, as it was closest to the garden) may have been part of this suite, but it is not clear. Jerusha's Sitting Room, mentioned by Mrs. Dadmun (to Lucie Welsh), was the first-floor old Howe Sitting Room (adjacent to the Parlor). Jerusha's suite did not have a fireplace, so Mrs. Dadmun's recollection might be accurate. After Jerusha's time, her bedroom became servant quarters. Rumors started in the 1990s that Jerusha's ghost appears in Room #9, but there is no evidence to support this claim.

Jerusha Howe's bedroom above the Old Kitchen. Ford-era photo. To the right are the stairs going down to the Old Kitchen area.

The Secret Drawer Society, not an organization per se but the term used by guests who participate in a casual ritual of writing small notes and inserting them in out-of-the-way places, shows up in this room (and just about every bedroom in the inn). It supposedly started around 1928, when guests found the secret compartment in the old Longfellow desk (then in the Parsons Bedroom). Small compartments were later found in other old pieces of furniture, and a very low-key communication forum started. There is no mention of it in any old magazine or the archives. It was very quiet or even nonexistent during the Koppeis era, but it seems to have blossomed in the 1990s.

Lafayette Bedroom

Lafayette supposedly stayed in this room, and his valet stayed in the small side alcove. It was the best overnight room in the house, and the most expensive. Most turn-of-the-century descriptions of the inn note the very old (over 150 years) "blue bells of Scotland" wallpaper that was once in this room. It was said that "the figure of the blue bell flower was stamped upon small squares of paper by hand, and square by square was laboriously placed upon the wall. The polished oak floors have been highly decorated with blue and brown flowers, painted in diamond checks."[69] A 1876 *Boston Daily Globe* mentions that when Mrs. Seymour gave a tour, one would get a souvenir of the room: "[The wallpaper]…which the zealous son of the household has torn bits to give you as mementos of the great Lafayette, who once looked upon it."

Lafayette Bedroom, Ford era, showing the "bluebells of Scotland" wallpaper (some of which was reproduced). Lafayette's valet supposedly used the small alcove room when the general was said to have stayed here (one of the inn's legends). In the Koppeis era, this was a museum room. Now it is used as a TV and sitting room for overnight guests.

This room was completely destroyed in the fire, but some of the floorboards with the original stenciling somehow were rescued. The floor was re-stenciled in the same pattern in the 1956–58 restoration. For years, it was a gated museum room, but this was relaxed by the 1990s. The room is now called the Howe Family Room, renamed as part of a deal to acquire the extremely valuable Howe family collection of papers donated in 1995. Most people still call it by its conventional name, the Lafayette Bedroom. It is currently the TV and game room for overnight guests.

Drivers' and Drovers' Room

This room was once called the Teamsters' Room, later the Washington Room (in 1895) and also the How Bedroom. The *Boston Traveler* of December 22, 1895 states, "In early times from 1740 to 1800, this room was occupied by Landlord Howe and his wife." (That would be Ezekiel, but this may not be accurate). It has also been referred to as the "Great Traveler's Room."

A Ford-era photo of the Edison Room (now the Drivers' and Drovers' Room). Ford named this room to honor his friend, and he furnished it to remind Edison of his boyhood home in Ohio.

This room was said to contain five beds, each of which was supposed to hold at least two individuals. Stage drivers, peddlers and common lodgers occupied them. A small stairway to the old Bar Room is in the corner of this room. During the tenant period, this room and the Lafayette Room were occupied, but the rooms across the hall were generally empty and filled with cobwebs and dust. In Ford's time, he honored his friend by calling this room the Edison Room (where Edison presumably slept when visiting).

Longfellow Bedroom

This is the bedroom upstairs on the southwest corner. Lemon and Ford called it the Longfellow Bedroom. Recently, the name changed to the

The Longfellow Bedroom during the Ford era.

Museum Chamber Room because in olden times, bedroom spaces were named for the room underneath them. Since the Parlor below is a museum room, it was so renamed. Since 1958, this has been one of the four (now three) museum rooms in the inn. Seymour tells us that this room was once split into three rooms with thin wood walls (but he tells us that was not original).

How Sitting Room (or How Family Sitting Room)

This is the room downstairs behind the Parlor. For over one hundred years, it was the How living room. Mrs. Dadmun, in the tenant period, referred to this as Jerusha's Sitting Room. Lemon turned it into a bedroom and called it the Washington Bedroom in tribute to the possibility that Washington rested in this room. This space was completely destroyed in the fire. When rebuilt, it was turned into a dining room (breakfast was served here in the Koppeis era). For a time in recent years, it was called the Back Parlor, but now it is back to being called the How Sitting Room.

Ford Room

In 1904, Lemon would attach the old woodshed on the property to the east wing. This became his private art gallery when renovations were finished in 1908 (see the picture in the Lemon chapter). When Ford owned it, it was his private bedroom. You can still find his maid call buttons in the woodwork. Now it is a large dining room.

The How Sitting Room. For over one hundred years, this was the How family living room. Lemon converted it into the Washington Bedroom. Now it is a small dining room. This is a Ford-era photo.

The Ford Room. This is an early 1920s picture showing Ford's bedroom. Ford's security guards patrolling around outside kept him awake, so he later moved into Jerusha's room. Formerly, it was Lemon's art gallery.

Lemon Dining Room

This room was originally called the Family Dining Room, or just the dining room. Lemon changed the name to the Washington Dining Room to pay homage to the fact that the general may have taken refreshments there. Ford later renamed it back to the dining room (or Old Dining Room, as seen on postcards). It was changed to the Lemon Dining Room in the early 1990s to try to discourage the Washington myth and also to pay tribute somewhere to Lemon. Legend and old house tour notes state that teamsters, drivers, farmhands and workmen were fed in the Old Kitchen. The Old Dining Room was where the meals were served for stage visitors and distinguished guests. Unfortunately, there is little evidence of the use of any of these rooms and how meals were served (other than noting that the noon meal was generally the largest meal of the day). The use of these rooms did move around over the ages, and guests, workers and family could very well have mingled in the old days. The little closet (pantry) to the right of the fireplace was for a long time the inn's telephone booth. To the left of the fireplace is access to the Taproom.

A 1930s-era picture of the Old Dining Room. Note the original Taproom in the rear.

Old Kitchen

Possibly part of the original structure of the house, this great room had often served as the inn's gathering place. Ford was said to have loved this room; he and Edison would sit by the fire on the wooden settee and talk. The fire was used for cooking, and it must have generated a massive amount of light and heat. It is no wonder the Hows wanted to stay in this wing—it likely was the warmest space. Today, the fire is natural gas fueled, and it has caused the room to lose much of its character. Newcomb tells us that the floor, paneling and mantel were replaced during the Lemon era. This room did not suffer much damage during the fire, though some of the wall panels were flipped to hide any blackening. Lemon had the display cabinet to the right of the fireplace built. He used this for his favorite antiques. The closet to

The Old Kitchen in the early 1900s Lemon era. The date this wing was constructed is unknown, and no records describe its use in olden days. The Old Kitchen survived the 1955 fire relatively intact, so it is now the oldest part of the inn.

the left of the fireplace was possibly the location of the first indoor bathroom in the inn. Long ago, there was also once a rear door off this room and a few sheds behind it. This may have been the fastest way to the family outhouse before the indoor facility was built.

Main Dining Room

Ford built the first main dining room in 1927–28. This room burned down completely (the fire started in the northern fireplace) and then was rebuilt in 1958 on the original stone foundation. It is the main hall for weddings, colonial balls and other larger gatherings. Under it is the full modern kitchen.

Taproom (the New One)

Built at the end of Ezekiel's era, the west wing Taproom was once the private How family kitchen and dining area. It was said that the ballroom above was built over a carriage shed, but there is no documented evidence the Taproom was ever this type of space. During the tenant period, this became a storeroom and indoor woodshed.

Ford called this the "Restaurant." Lemon called it the 1800 Dining Room. In the early 1960s, it briefly became the Red Horse Room when the bar function moved into this room from the Ford Room. In most of the Koppeis era, it was the Taproom and the center of the tavern's life.

In the far corner, nearest the road side, is the "lover's corner." Robert Frost once sat here with fellow poet David McCord and worked on his speech for John F. Kennedy's 1961 inauguration. R.S. Newcomb, Lemon's carpenter, mentions that he put a new front Dutch door in this room. Lemon wanted the ability to lock the lower part because he was "bothered by guests leaving by this exit and not paying their bills." The room now is a quaint dining space.

Rear Parlor/Front Desk

The area outside the main dining room where the front desk is now located was once the Rear (or Back) Parlor. The back door led to the old garden, where lilacs were planted. It might have been the main route to the icehouse, woodshed and perhaps the main building's outhouse. Lemon-era photos do exist of this once-wallpapered room; these show it to be a casual sitting space. This area of the inn was substantially modified when Ford built the large north wing. He turned the space into the hostess desk, which it has been ever since. It was renovated again in 1958 and in 2000.

Lower Hallway (A Walk through the First Floor)

Wallace Downes, in his *New England Magazine* article, describes entering the inn in 1887:

> Lifting the old-fashioned latch by a great brass knob, we pull open the heavy oaken door and turn down the wide hall-way, but are opposed in our passage by a large, wooden, five-bar gate. This gate divided the private from the public quarters. At the end of the hall on the left we enter what was the "family sitting room" of four generations of the Howe family. It is remarkable for nothing in particular except that its walls are covered with a curious kind of old-style wallpaper. Off this room is a long apartment which was utilized in getting up great dinners for special occasions. From the right of the hall we enter the "family dining room," which, like most of the rooms in the house, is of the square and low studded style. It is supplied with two spacious pantries, whose "good things" were kept from sight and whose appetizing odors were kept from the olfactory organ by the old-fashioned English double doors.

THE OLDEST OPERATING INN IN AMERICA

The days are short, the weather's cold,
By tavern fires, tales are told.
Some ask for dram when first come in,
others with flip and bounce begin.
—New England Almanac, *1704*

There are many claims to being the oldest in the business. Semantics of what is a tavern, an inn, a hotel, a restaurant or a bar play into the debate. Claims now also differentiate between "oldest" and "continuously operating." Another issue is that definitions change over time. Taverns historically were places where liquor and food were served, and outside of cities, they were generally places that also provided lodging for man and beast. The popularity of the word "inn" came later, influenced by the stagecoach, whose affluent customers wanted something seemingly more refined (later, "hotel" came into the vocabulary). Inns in England were places that provided accomodation, not just liquor, so here in America, the term seems to have been used to communicate extended services. It was up to the owner to decide what his place of buisiness was called, so "tavern" and "inn" became interchangeable (the name was not regulated).

Records show that past innkeeper Frank Koppeis researched these claims, penning letters to such places as Santa Fe, New Orleans, St. Augustine, Williamsburg, Jamestown, Philadelphia, New York and a few other old world places. None of these cities took credit as having any old and still-operating inns, taverns, bars or any type of house of entertainment older than the Wayside Inn.

There are a few in this country to note, however.[70] The White Horse Tavern in Newport, Rhode Island, claims "to be one of the oldest taverns in the country," which is a valid claim. It apparently was an old tavern, but it turned into a rooming house in 1875 and was not brought back as a restaurant and bar until 1957. They do say of themselves, "America's oldest tavern was originally constructed before 1673." The structure clearly is not of 1673 vintage; it has been rebuilt over the years. There are a number of buildings in Boston and other old world towns that were built on the site of old taverns (going back to the 1630s). I imagine if any one of these was converted to a tavern, it could "best" the White Horse's claim. The White Horse does have a recorded history going back to pre-Revolutionary times, so it is indeed one of the oldest taverns. Today, it does not lodge travelers as a colonial tavern would have in the past; it is a very nice restaurant and bar.

Similarly, the well-known Fraunces Tavern in New York City was opened as a tavern by Samuel Fraunces in 1762. It, too, had long stretches where it did not function as a tavern (it also burned down several times).

The Warren Tavern in Charlestown, Massachusetts, claims to be the oldest "tavern" in Massachusetts, but it is only circa 1780 and not a tavern proper. It is, however, very historic.

The Colonial Inn in Concord, Massachusetts, claims that a building existed on this site since 1716 but that it was not a tavern, inn or hotel. The innkeeping function started in 1889.

The circa 1776 Griswold Inn in Essex, Connecticut, claims it is "one of the oldest continuously operated inns in the country," which, subject to verification, seems a justified claim.

The Groton Inn, in Groton, Massachusetts, claims to date from 1678. Its history is not publically available (and it never seems to be written about), so this claim would need some validation. Unfortunately, the inn suffered a major fire in August 2011, and its future is uncertain.

The Beekman Arms in Rhinebeck, New York, with roots going back to 1766, when it was called the Traphagen Tavern, claims it is the oldest continuously operated inn in America. The only time it shut down was during World War II for a few weeks when rationing got in the way. The "oldest-continuously" might be a legitimate claim, but you'd have to ignore the lack of a barn and inability to service "beasts."

The Wayside Inn, a tavern starting in 1716, is still a tavern proper. To step above the tavern/inn definition debate, let us call it an inn, so it is the oldest-operating inn in America. If you add the 145 years of the Hows operating it as a tavern with the post-1897 operation (another 114 years), these 259 years still top the Beekman's 245 years and the Griswold's 235 years, so it can also claim to be the "oldest operated inn" in America. The Wayside's "continuously operating" gets affected by the roughly 36 years it was a rented country home from 1861 to 1897 (though it was still open to visitors).

CONCLUSION

I left the woods for as good a reason as I went there. Perhaps it seemed to me that I had several more lives to live, and could not spare any more time for that one.
—*Henry David Thoreau,* Walden

The story of the Wayside Inn reflects the story of our nation. Ford was right to deeply admire the men who founded this country and to want to know more about their "force and courage." The study of our past helps us reflect on who we are and what we should aspire to be. It was Einstein who once wrote so poignantly, "A hundred times every day I remind myself that my inner and outer life are based on the labors of other men, living and dead, and that I must exert myself in order to give in the same measure as I have received and am still receiving."[71]

As all of the past landlords came to understand, running the Wayside Inn is no small undertaking. A significant amount of time and resources are required to maintain the facility and to stay competitive. Today, the inn has a staff of 130 people and an operating budget of $5.3 million. Costs, regulations and exogenous factors continue to force the inn to adapt to the changing world and to find ways to increase its income as a nonprofit. This back-office work is the hard part. Most of us see just the front end—the warm fire, beautiful grounds, good food, pleasant atmosphere and all the cultural activities. Supporting the inn with business and donations is the only way it will continue as a public trust, owned and enjoyed by all of us.

So our story ends. We read of the indomitable will of John How, the forefather, and of his son Samuel, who acquired the land. The next How,

On the old Post Road, July 4, 2011.

David, would build the inn and receive the first license for a "house of public entertainment." His son (Ezekiel), grandson (Adam) and great-grandson (Lyman) later ran it. Longfellow touched the inn with the magic of a poet's pen and changed it forever. Lemon, Ford and others left their marks. Years later, a gallant midnight firefighting effort in freezing weather saved the inn from complete destruction. A well-researched and finely crafted restoration then put the inn back together, and Frank Koppeis came and brought it back to life. Our generation now has the privilege of adding more to the inn's remarkable history.

NOTES

PREFACE

1. You can't keep everything because it takes space and resource to manage; plus, keeping everything is impacted by another factor. Missing files in the archives, missing parts of the history, missing artifacts—the inn's records are filled with stories of pilfering. Rooms had to be cordoned off to keep people from handling and taking artifacts. We read very old accounts of portraits being stolen and piano keys taken for souvenirs. The inn's only copy of a picture of Jerusha Howe was stolen. The priceless Ephraim Smith gun used at the North Bridge once hung over the fireplace was stolen in the 1980s. In 1955, a significant number of prints and artifacts were stolen in the hours immediately after the fire. Notably, the rare Paul Revere prints in the Bar Room were lost for good. According to tradition, on July 16, 1776, Ezekiel How threw a party for the Town of Sudbury to read the Declaration of Independence in the Hobgoblin Room. The inn had the town's original copy—until it was stolen after the 1955 fire. When you read through the tour notes from former hostess Priscilla Staples, you get the impression that many Lemon- and Ford-era artifacts were still in the inn back in 1958. It seems most are no longer around. Stories are told of unscrupulous employees taking pewter and tea sets and visitors taking rare paintings and oriental carpets and trying to remove electric wall sconces. The students at the Boys' School built a real airplane, and that was stolen from their backyard. Even the retention of the objects in the archives now remains a security issue. We are lucky to have what is left, but some history has been lost.

INTRODUCTION

2. *Badger and Porter's Stage Register.* The stage register is in the archive collection of Old Sturbridge Village. No other years except 1829 were available. It lists Sudbury as a stop but does not mention the specific tavern where the stages stop. I excluded the one stop mentioned in East Sudbury.

3. The map labels the How Tavern as "Adam How's Hotel." An 1856 map owned by the Sudbury Historical Society also labels it as "Howe's Hotel." The 1830 map is in the collection of Old Sturbridge Village in Sturbridge, Massachusetts. Later, Hudson tells us in his 1889 history, "Sudbury was once home to five taverns along the Post Road." Hudson may have been talking about a time before East Sudbury (now Wayland) split off (1730) from Sudbury.

4. *Telegram*, "Longfellow's Wayside Inn."

5. Zed, "About the Wayside Inn."

6. Mann, "Remembers Other Days."

CHAPTER 1

7. Quoted in Rice, *Early American Taverns*, 23.

8. Hudson, *History of Sudbury*, 25.

9. Sargent, *Handbook of New England*, 43. He writes: "The 'Old Connecticut Path' first became known to the English from the Indians who brought corn from the Connecticut valley to sell in Boston. John Oldham was the first to traverse it and over it traveled the emigrants from Boston to settle at Windsor and Wethersfield. Starting from Cambridge, it followed the Charles River to Waltham, thence it went through Weston, Hopkinton, and Grafton into 'the Wabbaquasset Country' across the Connecticut line to Woodstock, reaching the Connecticut river opposite Hartford. The 'Connecticut Trail,' first noted by Winthrop in his journal in 1648, left the Old Connecticut Path at Weston and ran through Sudbury Center, Stow, Lancaster, and Princeton, through West Brookfield, Warren, and Brimfield, to Springfield. It avoided the hills, and is in part traversed today by the Massachusetts Central." I chose to use the well-researched Levi Badger Chase route for the Bay Path. This is roughly approximated on the map. (From Springfield to Oxford, below Worcester, it then runs through Hopkinton, South Framingham, Natick and Newton Upper Falls to Jamaica Pond. Other less reliable sources show the Bay Path on a more northerly route, running through Marlborough and Worcester.)

10. Coggeshall, "Nobscot and its Neighboring Hills." A more detailed account of Tantamous and his son, Peter Jethro, can be found in Temple's 1887 *History of Framingham*.

11. See Powell, *Puritan Village*.

12. Hudson, *History of Marlborough*, 26.

13. An erroneous statement in the 1929 Howe Genealogies points to a reference that does not exist (it states he might be a glover).

14. See a November 10, 1692 record in the state archives (47:107): "Act forbidding lewd and idle entertainment in Inns, taverns, alehouses, and victualing houses since these places were intended for the use of travelers and strangers who needed food and shelter, and for the use of poor people who were unable to provide adequately for themselves."

15. What is there now is a typical straight-faced Colonial two-story house, likely built sometime around the early 1800s but renovated recently. The American Antiquarian Society has a picture of the house in 1932 on its website.

16. Pointing out the hardships of the time, in a story much like that of Mary Rowlandson's 1675 Lancaster Indian captive saga, two of John Jr.'s daughters experienced similar trauma. On July 18, 1692, a party of hostile natives assaulted the house of a Lancaster man named Peter Joslin while he was laboring in the field. They butchered his wife, Sarah, daughter of John How Jr., three of their children and another woman living with his family. Elizabeth How of Marlborough, sister of Sarah and another daughter of John Jr., was also in the house visiting. She was said to be singing when the Indians broke in. Elizabeth and a fourth child of Mrs. Joslin's were carried into captivity. The child was murdered in the wilderness, but Elizabeth was kept captive for "three or four" years before she was finally "redeemed" by the government (Mary Rowlandson was captive for eleven weeks). Family tradition has it that Elizabeth's life was spared because the Indians were fascinated by her singing voice. She married and lived to the age of eighty-seven, but she never fully recovered from the shock.

17. No author specified. Document in the archives titled "Clipping from 'The *Times*,' October 11, 1888. 'The Wayside Inn, and Howe Inn-Keepers of Sudbury and Marlborough.'"

18. Hudson, *History of Marlborough*, 382–83.

19. Howe, *Genealogies*. It should be mentioned that there were seven How(e) progenitors in colonial America along with John, but it is not clear if John was related to any. They were James and Abraham Howe of Roxbury, Edward and Abraham Howe of Watertown (this Abraham we know came to Marlborough with John), Daniel and Edward Howe of Lynn and our John Howe of Sudbury. The Abraham Howe Tavern is mentioned in Bigelow, *Historical Reminiscences*, 192.

20. Sudbury Town Archives, http://www.sudbury.ma.us/archives, accessed August 10, 2011.

21. Massachusetts Judicial Archives, Middlesex County General Sessions Record Book 1686–1748, microfilm at the Massachusetts state archives.

22. Hudson, *History of Sudbury*, 69. While the general court issued in 1649, and confirmed in 1651, grants for the land in the "2 Mile Grant," technically the Indians had not yet signed the deed for the land. Peter Jethro, son of Tantamous, along with thirteen other Indian leaders, would sign this over in 1684. Hudson comments that these long delays have occurred elsewhere.

23. Interestingly, one of Samuel's thirteen children, Nehemiah (b. 1693), like his cousin Elizabeth, was also an Indian captive. This story takes place in New Hampshire back in 1747, when he was taken, then dragged to Canada. He died in a French prison in Quebec, but while in captivity, he wrote a narrative that was published in 1748 and again in 1904.

CHAPTER 2

24. Massachusetts State Archives, Ancient Maps and Grants, Third Series, vol. 37, 15. (A very similar 1708 map also exists [and was reproduced in Hudson's *History of Sudbury* on page 124], in vol. 4, 4.)

25. There is almost no information at all on when the first mill was built. We know it was a gristmill by 1744 because David mentions it in the deed to David Jr. One

very small lead on the original construction is a reference to an article appearing in the *Evening Gazette* on September 9, 1867, by a writer using the name "Zed." He speaks of a visit he made to the inn in the years after Lyman passed away. He was poking around, and at one point he was "sitting on the very chair the Squire used." In the drawers of the chair he finds some old papers. "One is leave for a 'Mil and Damm,' in 'ye first yeare of ye reighn of our sovereign Lord George King of Gt. Britain.'"

George I reigned from 1714 to 1727. The year 1714 is (probably) too early for the mill. George II reigned from 1727 to 1760. Based on this, 1727 might be the year of the mill's construction. This story was brought to my attention by the inn's miller, Richard Gnatowski. There is no mention that this was a sawmill. Likely, they fashioned the mill for food before they thought about lumber.

26. 1958 Hostess Notes by Priscilla Staples Rixmen (who was there throughout the reconstruction).

27. Massachusetts Judicial Archives, Middlesex Folio Collection, 1716-62x-4 (obtained through the Massachusetts state archives).

28. *Diary of Samuel Sewall*, 100.

Chapter 3

29. It is recorded everywhere as "1744/5," likely because it is difficult to read the actual agreement or possibly because of a later actual recording date.

30. A letter from E.J. Boyer to Miss Susan Dyer on September 17, 1931, attaches copies of these silhouettes. What happened to the originals is unknown. Later, in 1965, a relative of Miss Dyer gave a copy of the silhouettes back to the inn (and another hand-inked copy to the Sudbury Historical Association two years later). Along with the one of Ezekiel were silhouettes of his wife, Bathsheba, and of a grandson, Curtis. Ezekiel and Bathsheba face each other. Curtis was a grandson through their daughter Olive. The Ezekiel print is labeled Colonial Ezekiel How Jr., but this is believed to have been a mistake by Miss Dyer (Ezekiel Jr. was not a colonel, his wife was not Bathsheba).

31. Massachusetts Judicial Archives, Middlesex County General Sessions Record Book 1686–1748, microfilm at the Massachusetts state archives.

32. Hudson, *History of Sudbury*, 370.

33. Howe, *Genealogies*, 40.

34. Ezekiel How Jr.'s petition is preserved in the Framingham History Society.

35. His grave or tomb is marked on deeds, and there is a likely re-used burial vault just east of the house.

36. See the letter prepared by the historian of the National Trust for Historic Preservation.

37. Childs, "The Way-side Inn"; Nichols, "Extracts from the Diaries," 11. Lydia's comments are found in the chapter on Adam Howe. Isaiah states in his diary on January 1808: "Broke the Sleigh a few rods from Howe's at the Black Horse in Sudbury."

38. Mann, "Remembers Other Days."
39. Rogers, "Ahterton [*sic*] W. Rogers, cousin of Homer Rogers, says: I will gladly tell you what I know about the Wayside Inn and its people so far as I knew them."
40. Sudbury Town Archives, http://www.sudbury.ma.us/archives.
41. Middlesex Registry of Deeds and Probate Court Records, 208, for the original deed; Book 55, 379, for the transfer of the remaining property.

Chapter 4

42. These two drawings, along with a third one of their daughter Jerusha, were obtained on June 18, 1958, from Mrs. Alton Small of Marlborough, Massachusetts. Along with the pictures came a Fitchburg newspaper article on the inn, a list of creditors of the estate of A. Howe, Adam Howe's statement of payment of twenty-five dollars and a calling card of Mr. and Mrs. Adam Howe. Of these acquisitions, only the two pictures remain. What happened to the other objects, including the picture of Jerusha, is unknown.
43. Downes, "Wayside Inn at Sudbury," states almost the same.
44. Sudbury Town Archives, http://www.sudbury.ma.us/archives.
45. Abiel Winthrop was given $9,000 in his father's will (notes are in the archives); this seems to indicate that he was alive after 1840.
46. Schaick, *Characters in* Tales, 19.

Chapter 5

47. From a document titled "Productions of Agriculture in Sudbury" dated September 11, 1850. The cash value of Lyman's farm was $10,000, and Adam's was $9,000. This information is from Richard Gnatowski.
48. Parsons, *Old House in Sudbury*, 8.

Chapter 6

49. The gathering was held in Harmony Grove, Framingham, Massachusetts, on August 31, 1871. Over one thousand family members from all the Howe families attended the gathering, including Julia Ward Howe (of "Battle Hymn of the Republic" fame and a Howe by marriage). Julia even wrote a new song for the occasion (published in the gathering's pamphlet). The second day, those interested were invited to the inn.
50. Willie comes by years later to visit when Ford owns the inn. See the Hostess Diaries, August 12, 1929. The dates are from Willie's conversation with the hostess. The Lucie Welsh article says there were only two boys; Willie speaks of four. It had previously been thought that Orin moved out in 1878.
51. The Hostess Diaries, a daily record of the inn begun years later in 1929, mentions that a guest stopped by on September 4, 1931, who was a great nephew of Mead. He provides this story.

CHAPTER 7

52. The correct journal entry information comes from the archivist of the Craigie House in Cambridge, Massachusetts.
53. Longfellow, *Life of Henry Wadsworth Longfellow*, 72.
54. Drake, *Our Colonial Homes*, wrote in 1894: "During a visit made to the poet at his historic mansion in Cambridge, he talked very pleasantly of his first introduction to the 'Wayside' some thirty years before. Let the travellers of to-day who grumble at spending six hours on the road between Boston and New York take notice. The stage then left town at three o'clock in the morning, reaching Sudbury Tavern for breakfast, a considerable portion of the route being thus traversed in total darkness and without your having the least idea who your companions inside might be. It was under circumstances thus unprepossessing that he first made acquaintance with Howe's Tavern." The "some thirty year before" was Drake talking, and some thirty years before 1894 was 1862. Sudbury Tavern does not necessarily refer to the Wayside Inn (there was another tavern in town called this), and his friend Fields was with him in that dark carriage. Longfellow's comment was merely pointing out the conditions of a typical ride.

CHAPTER 8

55. 1896 newspaper, "Old Wayside Inn," Lemon archive box.
56. *Worcester Telegram*, "Ford Buys Famous Wayside Inn," 1.
57. Monti letter is in the archives.

CHAPTER 9

58. Zacharias, "Henry Ford and Thomas Edison."
59. In the later years, Ford was recorded to be at the inn for Thanksgiving 1935, interviewed at the gristmill in 1938 and there for the prewar interview in 1939. In 1940, he attended the chapel opening, and then in 1941, he came back for Muriel DeMille's wedding. He shows up again in December 1944, then not again until October 15, 1946, his last time there, as he died six months later. His grandchildren seemed to have stopped by the inn every summer on their way to Ford's Seal Harbor, Maine summer home.
60. On a tour of the South in 1925 to find a winter home, Henry and Clara Ford came across a depressed little town called Ways Station. It had surprisingly close characteristics to the Wayside Inn—a history of early exploration, Indian and colonial settlements, a connection to the American Revolution and the Civil War, plantation architecture and a historic fort (which Ford bought and restored). Like the Wayside Inn, Ways Station, later to be renamed Richmond Hills after Ford's estate, had a history that mirrored that of our nation.

Over the next twenty-two years, Ford bought eighty-five thousand acres, drained the swamps, constructed a sawmill, reconstructed the old fort, built a brick mansion, established Ford Farms to experiment in agriculture, subsidized healthcare and built schools, a church, a commissary, a trade school, a community house and homes for his six hundred employees. Ways Station was one of the most impoverished areas of Georgia. Ford sought to improve the quality of life and ultimately built 272 buildings on his property. With friends Thomas Edison and Harvey Firestone, Ford formed the Edison Botanic Society and conducted laboratory experiments, attempting to turn agricultural products into goods useful to the auto industry.

61. Letter from his daughter Katherine Brooks Norcross to the Framingham Historical Society, dated January 25 (no year).
62. Names involved in this original plan were found here: Garfield, "Sudbury, 1890–1989," www.sudbury.ma.us/services/news_story.asp?id=258.
63. Richards, "Four Verses of Poem," 1.
64. In 1854–55, James Garfield, nephew of the owner and later the twentieth president, was said to have taught school in this building.
65. See "America's Stories," Library of Congress, http://www.americaslibrary.gov.

CHAPTER 11

66. "Sudbury Town Reports," researched from 1891 to 1900 and 1910 by Lee Swanson for this book.

CHAPTER 12

67. *Boston Daily Globe*, "500-Year-Old Oak Tree," 8.
68. The barn that appears in the Clifton Church photo (possibly 1915) near where the garden is now located has the same cupola as the Puffer barn.
69. Downes, *Wayside Inn*, 26.

CHAPTER 13

70. Information on other inns obtained from their websites on August 10, 2011.

CONCLUSION

71. Einstein, *The World as I See It*, 1.

BIBLIOGRAPHY

BOOKS

Badger and Porter's Stage Register. Boston: Press of the American Traveler, 1829.

Bigelow, Ella A. *Historical Reminiscences of the Early Times in Marlborough, Massachusetts*. Marlborough, MA: Times Publishing Company, 1919.

Chase, Levi B. *The Bay Path and Along the Way*. Norwood, MA: The Plimpton Press, 1914.

Crawford, Mary C. *Little Pilgrimages Among Old New England Inns*. Boston: L.C. Page & Company, 1907.

Diary of Samuel Sewall: 1714–1729. Collections of the Massachusetts Historical Society. Cambridge, UK: Cambridge University Press, 1884.

Drake, Samuel A. *Historic Fields and Mansions of Middlesex*. Boston: James Osgood and Co., 1874.

———. "The Red Horse." In *Our Colonial Homes*. Boston: Lee and Shepard, 1894.

Earle, Alice Morse. *Stage Coach and Tavern Days*. New York: MacMillan Co., 1900.

Einstein, Albert. *The World as I See It*. London: John Lane, 1935.

Emery, Helen F. *The Puritan Village Evolves*. Canaan, NH: Phoenix Publishing, 1981.

Federal Writers Project. *A Brief History of the Towne of Sudbury in Massachusetts, 1639–1939*. Sudbury Historical Society. Reprint, 1968.

Forbes, Harriette M. *The Hundredth Town. Glimpses of Life in Westborough 1717–1817*. Boston: Rockwell and Churchill, 1889.

Frederick, Antoinette. "Wayside Inn Book of Facts." The Wayside Inn Archives. Unpublished, 2010.

Garfield, Curtis, and Ridley, Alison. *As Ancient Is This Hostelry*. Sudbury, MA: Porcupine Press, 1988.

Giora, Dana. *Longfellow in the Aftermath of Modernism*. St. Paul, MN: Graywolf Press, 2004.

Hotten, John C., ed. *The Original Lists of Persons of Quality 1600–1700*. London: self-published, 1874.

Howe, Daniel W. *Howe Genealogies*. Vol. 1. Edited by Gilman Howe. Boston: New England Historic Genealogical Society, 1929.

Hudson, Alfred S. *History of Sudbury, Massachusetts*. Sudbury, MA, 1889.

Hudson, Charles. *History of the Town of Marlborough*. Boston: T.R. Marvin and Son, 1862.

Longfellow, Henry W. *Tales of a Wayside Inn*. Boston: Ticknor and Fields, 1863.

Longfellow, Samuel. *Life of Henry Wadsworth Longfellow with Extracts from His Journals and Correspondence*. Vol. I. Cambridge, MA: John Wilson and Son, 1886.

Parsons, Thomas W. *The Old House at Sudbury*. Cambridge, MA: Press of John Wilson and Son, 1870.

Powell, Sumner C. *Puritan Village: The Formation of a New England Town*. Hanover, NH: Wesleyan University Press, 1963.

Temple, Josiah. *History of Framingham*. Framingham, MA, 1887.

Torrey, Bradford, ed. *The Writings of Henry David Thoreau, Journal*. Cambridge, MA: Riverside Press, 1906.

Rice, Kym, S. *Early American Taverns: For the Entertainment of Friends and Strangers*. Chicago: Regnery Gateway, 1983.

Sargent, Porter E. *A Handbook of New England*. Boston: Geo. H. Ellis, 1916.

Seabury, Joseph. *New Homes Under Old Roofs*. New York: Frederick A. Stokes, 1916.

Van Schaick, John, Jr. *The Characters in the* Tales of a Wayside Inn. Boston: Universalist Publishing House, 1939.

Whitcomb, Charlotte. "The Wayside Inn." In *The Book of a Hundred Houses*. Chicago: Herbert S. Stone & Co., 1902.

MAGAZINES

Arts and Decoration Magazine (October 1916).

Chenoweth, Mrs. Van D. "The Landlord of the Wayside Inn." *New England Magazine* 10, no.3 (May 1894).

Chidsey, Donald B. "The Old Boston Post Roads." *National Geographic* (August 1962).

Child Lydia M. "The Wayside Inn, The Howe Tavern in Sudbury as it Looked in 1828." *National Standard* (February 1872).

Church, J.C. "The Wayside Inn." *Bay View Magazine* 4 (March 1897).

Coggeshall, John I. "Nobscot and Its Neighboring Hills." *Middlesex Hearthstone* (June 1896).

Country Life in America (June 1902).

Downes, Wallace. "The Wayside Inn at Sudbury." *New England Magazine* 5 (1887).

Ford, Henry. "Why I Bought the Wayside Inn and What I Am Doing with It." *Garden & Home Builder* (July 1926).

"Howe Family Gathering, Harmony Grove, Framingham." *Welcoming Guide* (August 1871).

Lloyd, James L. "Longfellow, America's Poet Laureate." *Bay View Magazine* (March 1897).

Loring, Charles. "The Red Horse Tavern." *Garden & Home Builder* (July 1926).

Lunt, Adeline. "The Red Horse Tavern." *Harper's New Monthly Magazine* (September 1880).

Mead, Edwin D. "The Wayside Inn." *New England Magazine* (November 1889).

Seabury, Joseph S. "The Wayside Inn, Its Construction and Its Story." *The House Beautiful* (July 1914).

NEWSPAPERS

Associated Press. "Ford to Build Colonial Town." January 1925. [Also mentions Weare, New Hampshire wool-carding mill.]

Boston Daily Globe. "500-Year-Old Oak Tree Falls at Wayside Inn." April 17, 1959.

Boston Globe. "Pilgrims Reach Hub on Washington's *Boston Herald.* "Ford Party See The President and Swap Gifts." August 20, 1924.

Boston Journal (hand-transcribed letters to the editor), July 28, 1868; August 10, 1868; August 13, 1868; August 19, 1872 (date written); August 29, 1872. [Other hand transcribed references include a July 18, 1865 *Daily Evening Traveler* article, a July 19, 1865 *Boston Traveler* article and a November 20, 1897 *New York Times* article.]

Cash, William. "Friday Evening Dance Class Was High Spot of Wayside Week." *Boston Daily Globe*, March 7, 1947.

Colt, C.C. "Riding and Hunting, Millwood Hunt Takes New Lease on Life." *Boston Evening Transcript*, October, 1, 1924.

Globe (may be partial name). "Mine Host Ford Entertains at Diner in his Wayside Inn." February 12, 1924.

Journal [Southbridge, MA]. "The Wayside Inn." October 5, 1899.

A Journal of the Farm and Fi[nance]. "The Ancient 'Red Horse Inn' of Sudbury Struck by Lighting." August 15, 1868.

Lawrence, Charles A. "Red Horse Tavern, South Sudbury, Wayside Inn of Longfellow's Poem." *Boston Sunday Globe Magazine*, August 5, 1923.

Mann, William J. "Remembers Other Days of the Old Wayside Inn." *Boston Post*, August 18, 1923.

New York Herald Tribune. "Ford Says 'It's All a Big Bluff': 'They Don't Dare Have a War.'" August 29, 1939.

New York Times Magazine. "Wayside Inn Turns the clock Back." April 25, 1926.

New York Tribune. "The Wayside Inn." 1892.

"[Old] Wayside Inn which Longfellow Made Famous to be Reopened." 1896.

Post (may be partial name). "War Talk All Bluff Says Ford." August 29, 1939.

Richards, William. "Four Verses of Poem by Longfellow Moved Ford to Buy Tavern." *Detroit Free Press*, February 17, 1924.

Sudbury Town Crier. "Grist Mill celebrates golden anniversary." November 21, 1979.

Sunday Telegram. "Restoring Longfellow's Wayside Inn." December 16, 1923.

Telegram (may be partial name). "Longfellow's Wayside Inn." May 12, 1888.

Times (may be partial name). "The Wayside-Inn, and Howe Inn-Keepers of Sudbury and Marlborough." October 11, 1888.

Welsh, Lucie. "My Tale of Wayside Inn." *New Enterprise* [Norton], October 9, 1952. [A hand-written note on it says "refers to 1884."]

Worcester Telegram. "Ford Buys Famous Wayside Inn at Sudbury; May Maintain It for Public as Historical Museum." July 10, 1923.

Wright, Margaret B. "The Wayside Inn." *Christian Union*, February 10, 1887.

Zacharias, Patricia. "Henry Ford and Thomas Edison—A Friendship of Giants." *Detroit News*, August 7, 1996.

Notes, Letters, Speeches in the WSIA, Websites

American Antiquarian Society. "Photographs of Seventeenth and Eighteenth Century Structures in Massachusetts taken 1887-1945 by Harriette Merrifield Forbes." www.americanantiquarian.org/images/forbes/000420-0408.jpg.

Bent, Samuel. "The Wayside Inn-Its History and Literature." An address to the Society of Colonial Wars at the Wayside Inn, Sudbury, Massachusetts, June 17, 1897.

Boyer, E.J. Letter to Miss Susan Dyer regarding How silhouettes, September 17, 1931.

Bulluck, Helen, historian for National Trust for Historic Preservation. Letter to Ralph Carpenter regarding Washington and Lafayette's travels, April 14, 1958.

Burnett, Mr. Note written to the archives regarding cleaning dance hall and planning floors in 1871 or 1872, April 23, 1929.

Finan, W.H. Letter to Henry Ford regarding sleigh party, two maiden sisters, January 29, 1927.

How, Ezekiel, Jr. Petition for a pension to the Commonwealth of Massachusetts. Framingham Historical Society Records, August 1832.

Howard, Mr. and Mrs. Henry. Extract from special guest register regarding visit of first car to the inn (steamer in 1897), November 3, 1926.

Howe, Lyman. Account book covering the period 1846–57. From the 1995 Howe Paper collection.

Hugh, Mr. and Mrs. Rice, and E.P.L. "Visit to the Wayside Inn." Typed note, June 25, 1891.

Jenkins, S. *The Old Boston Post Road.* New York: G.P. Putnam and Sons, 1914.

Middlesex County Folio Collection. State Judicial Archives (microfilm in State archives) Columbia Point, Boston, MA. Folio 62x, 47:107, and microfilm labeled Middlesex County General Sessions Record Book 1686–1748.

Morse, Caroline O. "A Stopover at the Wayside Inn, Sudbury, Thanksgiving, 1860." Note sent to inn in the 1920s.

Newcomb, R.S. "Information Secured from R.S. Newcomb Who Made Alternations and Additions to the Wayside Inn During the Ownership of ER Lemon." Typed note, May 13, 1925.

Nichols, Charles L., ed. *Extracts from the Diaries and Accounts of Isaiah Thomas from the Year 1782 to 1804 and His Diary for 1808.* Worcester, MA: American Antiquarian Society, 1916.

Norcross, Katherine Brooks. Letter to the Framingham Historical Society regarding the Ezekiel How Jr. house, January 25 (no year).

Receipt of objects including the Adam Howe pictures, from Mrs. Alton Small of Marlborough, MA, June 18, 1958.

Reed, Charles. Letter to Henry Ford regarding suggestions for inn. Westborough Historical Society, September 26, 1923.

Rixman, Priscilla Staples. House tour notes. 1958.

Rogers, Atherton. "Ahterton [*sic*] W. Rogers, cousin of Homer Rogers, says: I will gladly tell you what I know about the Wayside Inn and its people so far as I knew them." Typed note, January 2, 1926.

Seymour, Horace C., and Lizzie Seymour. "Information secured from Mr. and Mrs. H.C. Seymour of South Sudbury, Mass. regarding the condition of the Wayside Inn prior to the changes which were made by Mr. ER Lemon former owner." Typed note to E.J. Boyer. Undated, likely 1923.

Sudbury Historical Society. "23 David How Dam and Original Mill Site." www.sudbury01776.org/tour.html.

Town of Marlborough. "The Lords of Whipsuppenike." www.marlborough-ma.gov/Gen/MarlboroughMA_Historical/settlers.

Whittemore, Florence. "The Wayside Inn." Letter read to her graduating class at Cambridge High School, July 19, 1865.

Zed (pen-name). "The Home Farm—The Red Horse Inn—The Howes. Correspondence of the *Gazette.*" *Evening Gazette,* September 9, 1867.

About the Author

B rian Plumb has had a close affiliation with the inn for well over twelve years. He is a fife player with the Sudbury Ancient Fife and Drum Company based at the inn, as well as a whistle and flute player with the Colonial Minstrels, the inn's resident colonial dance band. He performs there weekly. In 2009, he started the website howetavern.com to begin sorting and publishing his collection of material on the inn. Professionally, he serves as director of finance for a large energy company and holds an MBA and BSME.

Matt Brench, Brian Plumb, Diedre Sweeney, Al Petty and Joanna Brench of the Colonial Minstrels. *Photo by Russ Kirby.*